M & E HANDBOOKS

M & E Handbooks are recommended reading for examination syllabuses all over the world. Because each Handbook covers its subject clearly and concisely books in the series form a vital part of many college, university, school and home study courses.

Handbooks contain detailed information stripped of unnecessary padding, making each title a comprehensive self-tuition course. They are amplified with numerous self-testing questions in the form of Progress Tests at the end of each chapter, each text-referenced for easy checking. Every Handbook closes with an appendix which advises on examination technique. For all these reasons, Handbooks are ideal for pre-examination revision.

The handy pocket-book size and competitive price make Handbooks the perfect choice for anyone who wants to grasp the essentials of a subject quickly and easily.

D0620432

THE M & E HANDBOOK SERIES

Case Studies in Systems Design

R. G. Anderson
FCMA, MInst.AM(Dip), FMS

Senior Lecturer
West Bromwich College of
Commerce and Technology
Management Services Division

MACDONALD AND EVANS

Macdonald & Evans Ltd.
Estover, Plymouth PL6 7PZ

First published 1980

© Macdonald & Evans Ltd., 1980

7121 0387 2

Filmset in Monophoto Times 9 on 10 pt and
printed in Great Britain by
Richard Clay (The Chaucer Press) Ltd.,
Bungay, Suffolk

Preface

This book was written with two main purposes in mind. The first purpose is to ensure that students, and readers in general, gain an insight into practical everyday problems confronting businesses with regard to the design of business systems. The second purpose is to prepare students for examinations by means of case studies which cover many aspects of individual questions set in examinations relating to data processing, management information systems, business administration, office systems and mechanisation as well as systems design.

There is no universal agreement on the nature and format of case studies; one point of conjecture is whether case studies should provide solutions. This book does provide possible solutions or solutions which have actually been implemented to enable the reader who is not too conversant with the *modus operandi* of systems design to obtain an appreciation of the factors involved.

It is suggested that the reader attempts an outline solution to each case study when possible or when relevant, so that it may be compared with the solution provided; by this means omissions or misinterpretations can be noted. This in itself aids further understanding and further assists the learning process.

It is interesting that many examination questions take the form of mini-case studies. This is particularly relevant in respect of questions relating to the selection of alternative methods, decision tables, system flowcharts and computer-run charts.

This book could also be used on appropriate college courses where the case study method of teaching may be used to advantage.

A number of alternative approaches were possible for formulating the structure of this book. It could have been assumed that the reader already had sufficient knowledge of business systems and systems design to appreciate fully the nature of the problems contained in case studies, and was capable of generating possible solutions. If this approach had been adopted the book would have contained only case studies.

Another approach could have been the allocation of the first half of the book to matters relating to business systems and systems design in sufficient detail to provide a firm foundation for the reader to attempt solutions to case studies. This approach would have duplicated matters already dealt with in other books written by the author and indeed other authors.

The approach actually adopted is a compromise between those indicated above; that is, the steering of a middle course by providing a chapter on the nature of business systems and a chapter on the nature of systems design which may be supplemented by reference to other books written by the author which are complimentary to this book. The books referred to are also in the HANDBOOK series and their titles are: *Data Processing and Management Information Systems*; *Business Systems*; and *Organisation and Methods*. The remainder of the book is devoted to case studies and solutions.

The case studies contained in this book represent a cross-section of typical systems currently in use in a variety of industries including electrical appliances, structural engineering, steel manufacture and wholesale food distribution. With the exception of Case Study I which deals with a hypothetical situation developed by the author for reasons explained later, all the case studies depict actual situations.

The case studies embrace batch processing applications both by main frame computer and visible record computer as well as combined on-line and batch processing applications.

Each case study commences with an outline of the business environment and the circumstances leading to the need to develop new systems and concludes with an overview of what has been studied for the purpose of enabling readers to refresh their memories at the end of a case study. This is essential as it is so easy to overlook specific points of detail on a first reading; indeed, very little may be understood on a first run through.

The author has redrafted the case material kindly supplied by various organisations when appropriate, in order to present it in a more simplified manner for the less-initiated reader.

In general, the book would benefit students preparing for the examinations of the following bodies:

The Institute of Cost and Management Accountants (I.C.M.A.).
The Institute of Administrative Management (I.A.M.).

The Association of Certified Accountants (A.C.A.).

The Institute of Chartered Accountants (C.A.).

The Society of Company and Commercial Accountants (S.C.A.).

C.N.A.A. Degrees relating to business systems and systems design.

The HANDBOOK is also suitable for the requirements of the Business Education Council (BEC).

August 1979   R.G.A.

Acknowledgments

This book could not possibly have been written without the fullest co-operation and assistance of the organisations and individuals mentioned below, for which the author is profoundly grateful.

With regard to Case Studies II and III the author is extremely indebted to the directors of J. S. Forster & Co. Ltd. for giving their approval to the publication of details in respect of their payroll and labour costing applications. The author is also indebted to Mr E. E. Northwood, the Company Secretary of J. S. Forster & Co. Ltd. and Mr A. Wilkes, his assistant, for the time they placed at his disposal and for the kindly manner in which he was received and the assistance provided in sorting out the details of the case study material provided. The author is also grateful for the efforts of Mr D. Tennant of N.C.R. Limited for his introduction to J. S. Forster & Co. Ltd. and for granting permission to use system design material developed by N.C.R. Limited on behalf of J. S. Forster & Co. Ltd.

In respect of Case Study IV the author is greatly indebted to the directors of the company, which wishes to remain anonymous, and to the Data Processing Manager, Mr B. Perkins, for granting permission to use the systems material in respect of the order processing system. The author is also extremely indebted to Mr J. Worsey, Chief Systems Analyst, for the time he placed at his disposal for discussing specific aspects of the system and for demonstrating the operation of the system.

The author is also extremely grateful to Mr J. Webster, Systems Analyst/Programmer, for providing systems material in respect of his company's order processing system and for the time he placed at his disposal for discussing and demonstrating the details of the system in respect of Case Study V. Thanks are also due to Mr P. R. Burchell, Chief Accountant of the organisation concerned, which also wishes to remain anonymous, for permission to publish details of his company's system.

R.G.A.

Contents

Preface   v
Acknowledgments   viii

PART ONE: CONCEPTS AND PERSPECTIVE OF SYSTEMS DESIGN

I   *The Nature of Business Systems*   3
    Nature and structure of business systems;
    Classification of systems; Elements of business
    systems

II *The Nature of Systems Design*   15
    Environment of systems design; Change of me-
    thod; System objectives; Environmental factors;
    Identification of system problems; System prio-
    rities and standards of performance

PART TWO: CASE STUDIES

I   *Electrical Appliances: Raw Material Stock
     Control and Cost Control*   29
     General considerations; Preparation of block
     diagram and system flowchart; Description of
     computer runs; Checks and controls

II, III *Structural and Fabricated Engineering: Pay-
         roll and Labour Costing*   46
         II: *Hourly Paid Payroll*   49
         General considerations; Hourly payroll weekly
         processing routine; Payroll totals and note and
         coin analysis; General system requirements;
         Input proof sheet error corrections; Weekly
         salaries

         III: *Labour Costing*   70
         General considerations; Creation of contract
         labour cost master file; File amendments; Calcula-
         tion of check digits; Testing procedure; Weekly
         processing routine—data capture to cassette—
         general system requirements; Processing activities;
         Weekly processing routine—weekly updating of
         contract labour cost cards and weekly cost review
         report; Completed contracts routine

IV *Steel Making: On-line Order Processing and Related Sub-systems* 96

General considerations; Outline of order processing routine; Batch processing runs—further details; On-line planning; System master files; Outline of video screen and sub-routine functions; Video operating instructions; Sales orders and the sales accounting system—general outline; Sales accounting master files

V *Food Wholesaling: On-line Order Processing* 142

General considerations; General structure of the system; Processing routines; Data reports; System master files

Appendix Examination Technique 191

Index 193

PART ONE

CONCEPTS AND PERSPECTIVE
OF SYSTEMS DESIGN

CHAPTER I

The Nature of Business Systems

NATURE AND STRUCTURE OF BUSINESS SYSTEMS

1. Relationship of business operations and business systems.
Business organisation structures provide the foundations for conducting business operations, whereas business systems provide the means for effectively administering and monitoring such operations. Business systems support the whole spectrum of business operations including planning and launching a new product; planning production; paying wages; invoicing goods to customers; controlling stocks; scheduling aircraft; controlling holiday bookings; arranging insurance cover; controlling costs, income and expenditure; purchasing materials; order processing, and so on.

There exists a whole galaxy of business systems each of which is custom built to suit the operating characteristics of specific businesses which have a high degree of variety even within organisations in the same industry.

Factories process raw materials and produce saleable commodities or products whereas business systems process basic data relating to such operations, i.e. transaction data. Such data is used as input to the data processing system, which in a general sense most business systems are, for the purpose of calculating the wages of employees, producing sales invoices, purchase orders and updating of stock records, etc. In addition, business systems produce management information for the control of business operations, problem solving and decision making.

Data is normally recorded on source documents representing the activities and events that have occurred during the conducting of business operations. Data processing activities have assumed ever increasing importance in the last two decades which has necessitated the introduction of specialist data processing departments staffed by specialists. The specialists include systems analysts responsible for the design of business systems, and programmers who write the instructions for the computer to process data in a prescribed manner.

2. Men, money and machines. Business systems require resources to enable them to operate, in the same way that a factory or any other type of business activity requires resources. The nature of the resources are the same for any business venture or system. The most important resource is money for acquiring capital equipment (such as computers, V.R.C.s and typewriters) and for paying the wages of personnel operating the systems and for other operating expenses. Without money, the other resource requirements (men and machines) cannot be acquired.

3. Structure of business systems. Most business organisations are structured on a functional basis to facilitate administrative efficiency; to this end each function is controlled by a manager, such

TABLE I. BUSINESS FUNCTIONS AND SUPPORTING BUSINESS SYSTEMS

Function	System
Stores	Stock control
Production	Production planning and control
Purchasing	Processing purchase orders and invoices (Purchase accounting)
Sales	Credit control, order processing and invoicing (Sales accounting)
Accounting	Financial accounting including purchase ledger, sales ledger, nominal ledger and payroll
	Management accounting including cost accounting and budgetary control
Personnel	Recruitment, selection, training, and personnel services

as Chief accountant, Production controller, Production manager, Sales manager, Personnel manager or Stock controller. The various functional activities are supported by appropriate business systems as outlined in Table I.

4. System relationships. It must be appreciated that although business operations are functionalised for reasons explained above they are often related to each other either directly or indirectly and when designing systems it is essential to recognise the existence of these relationships. If the business operations themselves are related in some way it follows that the supporting business systems must also be related in a similar way.

Systems are often related by means of information flows whereby the output from one system is the input to another. Other interactions between systems may occur on what may be described as a chain reaction. For example, changes in the level of demand for various products affects the level of stocks required in the finished stock warehouse which, in turn, affects the quantities to be manufactured. This situation also reacts on the level of stocks required for raw materials and component parts, which affects the purchasing system, which must adjust economic order quantities and possibly amend forward orders to the new quantities.

It is this situation which often provides the basis for coupling systems (integration) to form a larger system. In other instances over-coupling causes unacceptable complexity as it becomes more difficult to define data relationships and report requirements (particularly with regard to their content and frequency) for the various managers concerned. This situation leads to administrative inefficiency. Each situation must be viewed in the light of circumstances, but failure to recognise system relationships and interactions can create sub-optimisation for the business as a whole. If, for instance, what is considered to be unnecessary information produced by one system is eliminated without its relevance to related systems being considered, then one system will be simplified but the other may cease to operate because it lacks the basic input to enable it to do so. For example, the cost office would not be in a position to record the wages cost of jobs or produce operating statements if the wages office failed to supply job tickets after producing the payroll.

CLASSIFICATION OF SYSTEMS

5. Types of systems. Various systems have different character-istics depending upon their nature; some may be classified as de-terministic, probabilistic, open loop, closed loop, open system, closed system, financial systems or information systems, etc. Whatever the nature of a system, it is imperative that it is dyna-mic or adaptive so that it is able to respond to change emanating either from internal or external environmental sources. This is essential in the modern business world because sociological, tech-nological, economic and legislative factors are undergoing con-tinuous change.

An individual business may be classified as a total system re-lative to the functions forming the business structure. The func-tions may be classified as sub-systems which operate interactively to achieve corporate objectives. Taking this consideration a stage further, the departmental procedures which together form the basis of a functional system may be defined as smaller sub-systems. These sub-systems (or sub-sub-systems) consist of com-binations of operations arranged in a logical sequence for the purpose of achieving specified requirements as efficiently as pos-sible.

6. Sub-systems comprising a wages system. A typical wages system, itself a sub-system of the accounting system, consists of the following distinct procedures:

(a) clock card procedure for calculating wages based on attended hours;
(b) piecework or job ticket procedure for calculating wages based on results;
(c) holiday credits and holiday pay procedure;
(d) P.A.Y.E. and deductions procedure including the prepara-tion of payslips and earnings and tax records which may be clas-sified as the payroll procedure;
(e) wages paying-out procedure;
(f) wages analysis procedure for cost and budgetary control and other statistical purposes.

7. Sub-systems comprising a sales accounting system. A sales accounting system may typically consist of the following distinct procedures:

(*a*) editing customer orders for correctness of item code and description;

(*b*) checking the credit status of existing and prospective customers;

(*c*) checking stock availability of items ordered;

(*d*) preparation of stock picking lists, dispatch documentation and routeing instructions;

(*e*) updating stock records in respect of items dispatched;

(*f*) stock replenishment procedure;

(*g*) preparation of invoices from dispatch note copies if appropriate;

(*h*) updating sales ledger with value of goods dispatched, remittances and adjustments;

(*i*) preparation of statements of account;

(*j*) sales analysis;

(*k*) profitability reports.

ELEMENTS OF BUSINESS SYSTEMS

8. Elemental framework of business systems. All business systems whether manual, mechanised or automated consist of the same basic elements: input, processing, output, storage and control. It is now proposed to consider each of these elements, as they are fundamental to the effective design of business systems.

9. Input element. Input to a business system is in the form of data which either relates to transactions which have already occurred, such as hours worked by employees in the previous week, or which are to occur, such as a customer's order requirements. The data consists of basic facts relating to business transactions, and these facts are normally recorded on a prime document referred to as a source document which in the examples indicated above take the form of a clock card and a customer's sales order.

The data on source documents may be dealt with in a variety of ways depending upon the method of processing in use. Various methods are listed below.

(*a*) Manual system. Data is read and interpreted by a clerk in readiness for processing in accordance with procedural rules.

(*b*) Visible record computer (V.R.C.). Data is read by the V.R.C. operator and keyed into the machine's internal memory by means of the machine's integral keyboard. Alternatively, in order to achieve faster input, the data may be first punched into paper tape, edge-punched cards or eighty-column standard punched cards. The data is then input by an appropriate input device.

(c) Main frame computer. If the technique of batch processing is employed it is necessary to convert data from human sensible source documents to machine sensible form, i.e. paper tape or punch card code. This is done by punch operators. The data is then input either by a paper tape or card reader. This is referred to as indirect input, as original data is not input without first being converted.

Some systems, however, employ direct input methods whereby data on source documents is recorded by magnetic ink or optical characters or marks. They are sensed by magnetic ink or optical character/mark readers and the coded signals are then input for processing. Systems employing on-line processing techniques input data directly from source documents by terminal keyboards, i.e. a V.D.U. or teletype. This eliminates the need for data conversion.

(d) Computer bureau. When a computer bureau is used for processing business data the data is normally recorded on input forms provided by the bureau. Alternatively the bureau may be supplied with the original source documents or pre-punched tapes or cards.

10. Processing element. This element is concerned with converting a mass of obscure detail into a meaningful form involving the validation and sorting of data into a related logical sequence, calculating values, summarising values, updating records and printing documents and reports. The precise nature of processing operations is dependent upon the nature of the application as shown by the two examples in Table II.

11. Storage element. The term storage relates to the retention of various types of records either for updating or reference purposes. A series of related records combine to form what is referred to as a master file. Master files may contain records relating to customers' or suppliers' transactions thereby providing the basis for maintaining control over the current status of each record on the file. This enables the current balance outstanding on a customer's account to be compared with a predefined credit limit as a basis for credit control. Similarly, the balances on suppliers' accounts provide a means of establishing how much is owed to each of a company's suppliers.

TABLE II. PROCESSING OPERATIONS

Application	Operations
Wages system	Validate data and compile control totals
	Sort wages data to employee clock number sequence within department
	Calculate gross wages
	Calculate tax and other deductions
	Update wages file
	Print payslips and payroll
Sales system	Validate data and compile control totals
	Sort order details to stock number sequence
	Price and calculate value of items ordered
	Calculate V.A.T.
	Update stock file
	Sort order details to customer number sequence
	Update customer file
	Print invoices

Of particular importance to systems design is the type of master file required for reference purposes during processing.

As an example, an on-line order entry system will need to access a product file to obtain product descriptions when the terminal operator inputs item codes from sales orders. Similarly, a customer file will require accessing to obtain the addresses of customers or account balances when the terminal operator inputs account numbers.

In other instances it will be necessary to access a rates file when calculating wages and a materials file for obtaining material prices when stock updating and calculating the value of issues to production. In airline booking systems, information in respect of specific flights is accessed when a flight number is keyed in on a terminal.

The nature of the files used in various types of system are summarised in Table III.

TABLE III. TYPES OF FILES

System	Nature of files
Manual	Loose leaf ledgers Ledger cards
Visible record computer	Ordinary ledger cards Magnetic ledger cards Magnetic tape cassette Edge-punched cards Magnetic tape Paper tape Punched cards
Main frame computer	Magnetic tape files for high capacity, serial access, high-hit-rate applications Magnetic disc files for direct access and/or low hit-rate applications

12. Output element. Output is the final product of data processing activities which often takes the form of basic documents supporting business transactions such as sales invoices and statements of account regarding sales to customers, payslips in respect of employee earnings and purchase orders with regard to supply requirements.

Other forms of output consist of schedules or summaries relating to items in stock, i.e. a stock schedule or employee earnings and deductions (or payroll). An extremely important type of output is management information and the designer of systems must be certain of the exact needs of management. Information, to be worth its salt, must serve a useful purpose, and this is satisfied if it enables managers to be more effective in the control of key elements in their sphere of responsibility. The nature of this type of output takes many forms depending on the type of business but examples of typical reports include:

- (a) contract cost reviews;
- (b) customer turnover reports;
- (c) cost variance reports;
- (d) aged analysis of account balances;
- (e) product profitability report;
- (f) accounts exceeding credit limit;
- (g) excess stock report;
- (h) utilisation of resources report.

The output from a system is often in the form of hard-copy, i.e. printed reports; but this may not always be necessary particularly with regard to management information. A system provided with direct access facilities enables a manager to access information from a computer's files when required. This information may be displayed on the screen of a V.D.U. in a transitory manner. This sophistication dispenses with the need for a printed report in many instances and so assists in reducing the flow of paper-work in a business. What is more important, however, is that a manager can gain access to information when he needs to, rather than have to wait for reports to be provided at pre-defined intervals (which is a feature of batch processing applications).

13. Control element. When designing business systems it is essential to specify specific checks and controls to be incorporated in them. The types of checks and controls to some extent is dependent upon the processing method to be used which, at the present time, is either a micro, mini or main frame computer. Particular types of controls and the methods to which they are normally applicable are outlined in Table IV.

There are, of course, many other checks and controls which may be built into business systems particularly when using a main frame computer. These include checks to ensure that data is of the correct type, for the correct period, in the correct sequence, has the correct number and type of character in each field

TABLE IV. CHECKS AND CONTROLS

Control factor	General outline	Method of processing applicable
Check digit verification	Additional digits are included in reference numbers such as account, stock, employee, job, contract or operation numbers to ensure that data in respect of business transactions is recorded on the correct records. Invalid numbers are rejected.	V.R.C. Main frame computer
Hash totals	Typical hash totals may consist of an account number and account balance or the sum of daywork hours and piecework value. Such totals are to ensure that correct amounts are input and correct records posted depending upon the type of hash total used. The hash total entered by the operator is compared with a machine calculated hash total. Any difference indicates an input error. Provision must be made either to reverse incorrect entries, to reject entire records or to correct hash totals.	V.R.C. Main frame computer
Batch totals	To ensure that all items have been posted it is customary to prepare a pre-list of items in a batch. During processing specific values are accumulated which pro-	V.R.C. Main frame computer

TABLE IV.—*contd.*

Control factor	General outline	Method of processing applicable
	vide a batch total when the batch is fully processed. The total is compared with the pre-list batch total for the purpose of indicating any difference which may be caused by omission of an item(s), i.e. an incomplete batch has been processed. The missing item(s) must then be located.	Keyboard accounting machines (electro/ mechanical)

and that the correct generation of master file is being used for updating. It is also necessary to ensure that data conforms to a stated range of values; items which fall outside the range are signalled for validation.

As business data is largely processed by computer it may be useful to the reader to appraise the five elements in respect of a main frame computer system.

14. Elements of a computer system. The five elements may be summarised as follows.

(*a*) Input. Data is input for processing by means of an appropriate input device which may be a card reader, paper tape reader, optical character reader or visual display unit (V.D.U.), etc.

(*b*) Processing. The operations to be performed on data are carried out by the central processing unit (C.P.U.), which has electronic circuitry for performing arithmetical and logical operations. Processing is performed automatically by means of an internally stored program.

(*c*) Storage. Master files are normally stored on magnetic media (tapes or discs). Master files contain records of transactions relating to sales, purchases and wages, etc.

(*d*) Output. Printed output is produced by a line printer or may be displayed on a V.D.U. screen.

(e) Control. Processing operations are automatically controlled by a program, in conjunction with the operating system and control unit. The computer's operations are also controlled by a console typewriter.

CHAPTER II

The Nature of Systems Design

ENVIRONMENT OF SYSTEMS DESIGN

1. System design. The process of designing business systems embraces both the design of new systems and the redesign of existing systems. New systems are required when businesses first come into existence for administrative purposes. Existing systems need to be redesigned periodically to ensure that they accord with current, and not historic, administrative requirements. This is essential to maintain business efficiency.

2. Need for co-operation. Systems cannot, and must not, be designed without enlisting the aid and co-operation of user (operating) department staff, and to this end the staff concerned with the system under consideration should be co-opted to the study team. This approach ensures that the experience they have gained in operating the system, perhaps for a considerable period of time, is reflected in the design of the new system. The staff will be in a position to inform the system designers of the significance of seemingly trivial operations, the shortcomings and strengths of the system and, what is more, the real needs of the system.

System designers should appreciate that they are providing a service to the operating departments to enable them to operate more efficiently and not merely designing systems for the purpose of assessing their own ingenuity. This is not to say that ingenuity is not required, indeed it is; without it business would be suffering from inferior systems or trying to operate technically excellent systems which are too complex for comprehension by operating staff—the users of the system.

3. Approach to systems design. Because systems design is a creative activity, it requires a breadth of experience of how systems are structured and the purpose which they serve within the overall business environment. It is essential to adopt a panoramic outlook rather than a close-up snapshot approach; otherwise an incorrect, or too narrow, perspective will be obtained with regard to system relationships. This requires the "systems approach" to avoid systems being designed in isolation to each other because this leads to sub-optimisation for the business as a whole.

The approach of a designer of business systems must also be similar to that of a design draughtsman concerned with designing saleable products such as washing machines or automatic tea-makers. He must first of all establish the cost the market will accept, the standards of performance acceptable, design structure (which must be as simple as possible), ease of maintenance and reliability. It is also necessary to consider operating costs. These factors equally apply to the design of business systems because it is hardly feasible to design a system which achieves the basic requirements if it costs too much to implement and operate. This could apply when a costly computer is implemented when all that is necessary is a microcomputer.

Before embarking upon a systems development project the terms of reference must clearly define system demarcation lines (limits to the assignment); otherwise the systems of the business as a whole could be redesigned because of their interdependence and interrelationships (*see* I, **4** and Case Study IV).

4. Purpose of systems. Before embarking upon the design of a system it is mandatory for a system designer to establish the *raison d'être* of the proposed system because without this know-ledge it is not possible to ascertain the key elements on which to base the design of the system or even to decide whether it is necessary at all. A system should be initiated or remain in exist-ence only if it can be proved that it serves a useful purpose. A system without a useful purpose should not remain in existence because it utilises resources which could be employed to greater advantage in other operations of the business.

Systems often outlive their initial purpose, in which case they should either be modified or discontinued so that they accord with current and not historical business needs.

CHANGE OF METHOD

5. Reasons for change of method. The design of any business system necessitates, among other factors, an analysis of the basic operations to be performed which are the same whatever the method of performing them whether by a clerical system, mini or main frame computer. What is different is the method of doing them, which can be manual, electronic or even mechanical.

Due to business growth or changes in the structure of the business a change of method may be necessary for efficiency and cost effectiveness. Very often major changes in the volume of data to be processed necessitates a rethink in respect of the method of processing to be adopted. With regard to increasing volumes of data this may necessitate changing from either a clerical method to a V.R.C.; V.R.C. to an in-house main frame computer or computer bureau or even to a larger main frame.

A particular instance known to the author concerned a business which changed from a punched card installation (now obsolete) to a main frame computer for various applications. Subsequently, the business was taken over by a company which already operated a larger, more powerful computer. The situation was then reviewed with regard to the methods of data processing that then existed in the group. The result was that the smaller computer was disposed of and a key-to-disc system installed in its place. This system was used for preparing data for transmission to the central computer instead of processing it locally. No doubt data processing rationalisation and cost effectiveness as well as efficiency were borne in mind.

6. Determining the most suitable method. In general it is necessary to take a number of factors into account before deciding which is the most suitable method to apply in the prevailing circumstances. It must be appreciated that some methods will be superior to others but perhaps too sophisticated for the real needs of the business. In any event the more sophisticated the hardware the higher are the capital costs, so it is essential to consider both the suitability of particular machines and their cost before coming to a decision.

Other factors to consider include:

(*a*) the volume and frequency of transactions to be processed—both the average situation and peak loads;

(*b*) system response time requirements;

(*c*) the extent to which systems require to be integrated;

(*d*) the geographical dispersion of business operations;

(*e*) the volume and frequency of information and other output requirements;

(*f*) the frequency of file reference;

(*g*) the number of records in master files.

7. V.R.C. vs. main frame computer. It is now proposed to provide a brief résumé of some of the important differences between a V.R.C. and main frame computer, to assist the reader in his deliberations when attempting solutions or understanding the reasons for the choice of method in respect of the various case studies. It may be accepted that a V.R.C. is a small electronic computer mainly suitable for the smaller business, probably those presently using an obsolete electromechanical keyboard accounting machine for its accounting routines. Such a business will have a smaller volume of transactions to process than a larger business, which does not warrant the capital outlay and operating costs associated with a main frame computer. Some of the important differences of a V.R.C. are outlined below.

(a) It does not require a critically controlled environment—it may be installed in any suitable office.

(b) Highly trained computer operators are unnecessary; the main requirement is an operator with high keyboard dexterity.

(c) A powerful V.R.C. costs much less than a small main frame computer.

(d) A V.R.C. usually has a much smaller internal storage capacity.

(e) A V.R.C. has a lower speed of input but this may be increased by automatic input devices.

(f) Programs for a V.R.C. are usually developed by the manufacturer; therefore the user does not have to employ programmers.

8. Batch vs. on-line processing. When a decision has been made to implement a main frame computer it must then be established whether batch or on-line processing is most relevant to the needs of the business.

Batch processing is concerned with processing batches of related data for defined periods of time. The main reason for adopting batch processing in most businesses is economy as many businesses have high volume routine data processing requirements which are adequately served by automatic input and output devices that operate with a minimum of manual intervention under the control of application programs.

Batch processing operations are often used for payroll, stock control, invoicing and sales ledger, purchase accounting and the nominal ledger, etc. Unless a systems response time requirement is critical this technique of processing is quite adequate in many instances, but there is a tendency at present for many data processing systems to be improved by utilising on-line processing.

On-line processing requires terminals to be connected directly to a processor by means of cables, telegraph or telephone lines. This type of processing provides direct updating facilities whereby files are adjusted with current transaction data by means of terminal keyboards. Direct access to information stored in backing files is also possible; this enables key facts to be obtained when required rather than when they become available, as is the case with batch processing (*see* I, **12**).

Data preparation or conversion operations are dispensed with when using on-line processing; this reduces the time required to get data into the system.

Some on-line processing systems deal with transactions as they occur on a continuous processing basis instead of collecting similar transactions in batches and processing them together. This is referred to as transaction processing. Not all on-line systems process transactions in this manner because some highly interactive on-line processing operations are often supported by batch processing operations. This may be instanced by Case Study IV dealing with on-line entry of order details supported by daily and weekly batch processing routines relating to the production of works and customer documentation, invoicing and file updating, etc.

In other instances similar operations may be dealt with completely on a transaction processing basis, e.g. when a customer's order is received, a terminal operator interrogates the computer system's product file to check stock availability. The credit status of the customer can also be checked in a similar manner. This can be done while the customer is on the telephone if necessary. If the order is accepted and stock is available, the computer validates the input data by means of a data validation program and then proceeds to print dispatch documentation and invoices for the goods dispatched. The customer's account will then be updated on the sales ledger file and the relevant stock records on the stock file will also be updated. Each transaction is dealt with by all relevant processing operations before proceeding with the next transaction. With batch processing all transactions in a batch are dealt with as a group by individual processing operations such as validation, sorting and calculating, etc. before proceeding to the next operation.

Batch processing is a typical processing technique applied to many accounting routines whether processed manually, mechanically (accounting machine) or electronically (main frame computer or V.R.C.), but on-line processing only applies to more sophisticated computer configurations.

SYSTEM OBJECTIVES

9. Corporate objectives. In order to ensure that systems under development conform with corporate requirements it is essential for systems designers to have a clear and unambiguous appreciation of the objectives of the business as a whole. Only in this way will unity of direction be achieved. If this factor is not taken into account, systems will be out of balance with each other on the one hand, and out of phase with the real needs of the business on the other. In both cases corporate objectives will fail to be achieved.

A designer must be aware of the economic purpose of the business, the types of products marketed and the markets aimed at before he can be in a position to assess the relevance of the objectives of individual systems. The objectives of particular systems are not simply assumed by the system designer; they are established by discussion with management, who must agree to them before system design gets under way. Objectives should, whenever possible, be specified in meaningful quantitative terms. It is then possible to monitor system performance by comparing actual results with planned performance, thereby providing the basis for managerial control.

Corporate objectives may be broadly defined as follows:

(*a*) achievement of a specified rate of return on sales;

(*b*) achievement of a specified rate of return on assets;

(*c*) achievement of a specified rate of annual growth in respect of sales, earnings per share, market value of shares;

(*d*) maintenance of existing capital gearing ratio;

(*e*) reduction of the cost of all products;

(*f*) increase of the profitability of specified product groups;

(*g*) elimination of products with a contribution less than a defined amount per unit;

(*h*) increase of the market share of specified products;

(*i*) increase of the turnover rate of stocks and W.I.P.;

(*j*) development of new markets—home and export;

(*k*) improvement of customer satisfaction with respect to

price, quality, delivery, credit terms and after-sales service;

(*l*) improvement of cash flows.

10. System objectives. The objectives of particular systems must be determined within the framework of corporate objectives as indicated above. Production planning systems must ensure that production flows smoothly to achieve a given utilisation of assets; so that a higher level of production facilitates a higher level of sales and a higher level of profit, which achieves a higher rate of return on assets employed in the production process. This factor is also the basis of achieving a specified rate of annual growth in respect of sales—assuming, of course, that all production is capable of being sold. If production bottlenecks are removed then the turnover rate of W.I.P. is increased and a reduction of product costs is possible because a higher level of production reduces the fixed costs per unit. This assists in attaining increased product profitability.

The objective in respect of customer satisfaction is partly satisfied by efficient production planning, because as a result of this delivery promises are more likely to be fulfilled. Customer satisfaction may also be achieved by an effective sales accounting system which ensures that customer orders are dealt wiith efficiently and special orders notified to the product design office without delay. Improved cash flows may also be achieved by speeding up the preparation of invoices and statements of account.

Marketing systems also have an important part to play in developing new markets, improving after-sales service, developing an effective pricing policy and ensuring that orders are received for the most profitable products.

ENVIRONMENTAL FACTORS

11. Corporate profile. The particular significance of a system can only be judged within the framework of the business as a whole and for this purpose it is necessary to identify the environmental factors affecting the business and to assess those likely to affect the performance of particular systems. Accordingly it is appropriate to formulate a corporate environmental profile analysing both internal and external factors.

12. Internal environmental factors. The internal framework of a business can be outlined by listing specific factors as follows:

(*a*) type of product manufactured and sold or merely distributed as in the case of a wholesale food warehouse;

(*b*) type of market—whether home, export, wholesale, retail, consumable or capital;

(*c*) share of the market obtained;

(*d*) state of labour relations;

(*e*) quality/cost effectiveness of the products;

(*f*) profitability of the company compared with other companies in the same industry;

(*g*) liquidity of the company;

(*h*) turnover rate of assets in relation to sales;

(*i*) sales turnover;

(*j*) discount policy;

(*k*) credit policy;

(*l*) types of process;

(*m*) main functions;

(*n*) stock policy;

(*o*) investment in research and development;

(*p*) organisation structure—grouping of activities/centralised-decentralised operations.

13. External environmental factors. The external framework of a business from which threats and opportunities arise may be outlined by listing specific factors as follows:

(*a*) main competitors' share of market;

(*b*) new market opportunities;

(*c*) national economic growth rate compared with internal growth rate;

(*d*) state of labour market;

(*e*) possible threats to continuity of supplies in respect of crop failures or political issues;

(*f*) technological developments and their likely effect on the business;

(*g*) trends in the rate of inflation;

(*h*) world economic climate;

(*i*) trends in demand and consumer preference;

(*j*) likely level of interest rates—cost of funds for investment projects;

(*k*) impending government legislation.

IDENTIFICATION OF SYSTEM PROBLEMS

14. Current systems. A high degree of design activity is concerned with the redesign of existing systems, often because they contain problems which impair operational efficiency. In such cases it is necessary to identify the problems and then determine how to overcome them. This takes place during the analysis stage of a system designer's activity and he will soon learn about these from the operating staff. Problems often take the form of input delays, processing bottlenecks, lack of communication, insufficient information or lack of control. The following section identifies typical problems.

15. Typical system problems. The details which follow are merely representative of the specific problems which particular systems may possess:

    (*a*) credit checks take too long;

    (*b*) stocks are out of phase with changes in demand;

    (*c*) invoicing is delayed too long after goods have been dispatched;

    (*d*) out of stock situations are not reported early enough;

    (*e*) profitability of sales report is delayed too long after the end of the operating period;

    (*f*) production batches are too small for the level of productivity required;

    (*g*) stocks are not turned over frequently enough—investment is too high;

    (*h*) input is not transferred to wages office for wages calculation early enough;

    (*i*) wages take too long to calculate by the present method;

    (*j*) special production orders are received too late to achieve delivery promise;

    (*k*) there is difficulty in determining discount for particular situations.

SYSTEM PRIORITIES AND STANDARDS OF PERFORMANCE

16. Priorities. All systems must be designed in such a way that priority situations are dealt with in a prescribed manner otherwise they will fail to operate effectively, if at all. In an order processing application for instance, new receipts into stock must be allocated in the first instance to back-orders, i.e. those orders which previously suffered from shortages. Similarly, in a manufacturing environment if a number of orders have the same priority ranking, a further priority ranking can be established whereby orders which have already been started will have a greater priority than those which have not—the nearer an order is to completion, the greater its priority.

As an additional example, when computer based systems are designed to operate in batch and real-time mode concurrently, a system of priorities must be established so that real-time messages have preference over batch processing jobs. This will necessitate temporary halts to jobs running on a batch processing basis to deal with real-time requirements. There are even instances when different classes of real-time messages have a different priority rating so that a priority interrupt can be interrupted by a higher rated requirement.

17. Standards of performance. It is essential to determine the standards of performance required in respect of each system as a prerequisite to the effective design of such systems. Standards of performance provide a framework on which to evolve the best system within the prevailing circumstances. Standards also provide the framework for monitoring the results obtained and establish a basis for the achievement of system objectives. Some standards of performance of a general nature are outlined below.

(a) Systems must be so designed that they operate smoothly, consistently and effectively and attain the required objectives.

(b) Systems must remain in phase with the environmental changes taking place, i.e. they must be capable of responding to change, which means that they must be dynamic and not static.

(c) Systems must be designed so that they achieve the desired response time needs of the situation and accordingly business transactions must be dealt with in an adequate time scale. There is something wrong with a system if, for instance, the status of seats on a flight cannot be indicated immediately. Similarly, a delay of twenty-four hours in reporting a stock shortage is unacceptable especially in a wholesale warehouse or spares supply organisation. It is this factor which often determines whether a batch or on-line system is relevant.

(d) A system must process data at an acceptable level of accuracy suitable to the circumstances prevailing in specific systems which means the system must be capable of detecting and signalling the presence of specific types of errors in data.

(*e*) Systems must be capable of providing management with essential information at the right time.

(*f*) Systems must achieve budgeted operating costs unless there is good reason for them to be exceeded.

PART TWO

CASE STUDIES

Electrical Appliances: Raw Material Stock Control and Cost Control

GENERAL CONSIDERATIONS

1. Introduction. This first case study is a hypothetical situation based on a practical set of circumstances which may apply to any number of businesses. The case study was designed by the author in an uncomplicated manner so that it may be used as a basis for reasoning and as a means of providing a foundation for the study of actual cases in this book which, of necessity, are of a more complex nature because they depict the real world situation.

2. Type of business. The Amps and Volts Electric Co. Ltd. is in a highly competitive industry manufacturing household electrical appliances such as electric kettles, irons and fires. There is an increasing demand for kettles and irons but fires are subject to seasonal fluctuations. Batch production methods are applied for the manufacture of parts but assembly flow lines are installed for the assembly of appliances.

3. Current system and management requirements for proposed system. The business operates a clerical stock control system for raw materials which provides for daily updating of the stock file. The system also produces a monthly stock schedule showing the quantity of each item in stock. This schedule is considered to be inadequate because management also require to know the value of each item. In addition, management would like details of stock movements in respect of receipts and issues to be shown on the schedule which is required on a daily basis—not monthly as at present.

It is envisaged that the volume of transactions will increase in the future, due to a proposed expansion of the range of products to be manufactured and increasing demand of existing products, necessitating an increase in the range of materials to be stored. Management also require a more efficient method of dealing with stock replenishment because at present items are often found to be out of stock because of stock clerks failing to observe items which have fallen to the re-order level. This situation causes production delays and the associated costs of idle facilities. Very often higher prices have to be paid for obtaining emergency supplies from other sources than the normal supplier.

Management would also like any proposed system to provide a raw material product analysis each week indicating the value of issues chargeable to products to improve efficiency of the costing system.

Any proposed system must also provide a list of transactions for audit trail purposes. Check digits are also required to ensure the system rejects invalid raw material and product codes.

Details of volumes of transactions are as follows. Issue notes are presented to the stores each day from each of ten departments. The number of issue notes each day from each department is, on average, 200 but can be as high as 300. Each issue note contains an average of three items. The daily total of issue notes is usually 2,000, with a maximum of 3,000.

It is anticipated that the volume of issue notes will increase to about 250 a day, with a maximum of 400 a day in respect of each department. On average, 200 goods received notes (G.R.N.) are compiled each day but can be as high as 250. A separate G.R.N. is made out for each item received.

It is anticipated that the volume of G.R.N.s will increase to the average figure of 250 a day, with a maximum of 325.

At present the stock file contains 2,000 raw material records and this is expected to increase to 2,100. On average, one record in three is accessed for updating, i.e. the file activity ratio is 1:3.

It is considered that the work load will exceed the present capacity of the clerical system and it is not considered feasible to increase staff numbers as a more efficient method of stock updating and reporting is required.

The business already has a computer installed which is used for processing the payroll, sales invoicing, sales ledger and purchase ledger. It has sufficient spare capacity for the stock application and it is the policy of the board to computerise all suitable applications with a view to systems integration within the next five years.

4. Computer configuration to be used for proposed system. The computer configuration consists of:

    (a) card reader with a reading speed of 300 cards a minute;

    (b) central processor with a storage capacity of 32 K bytes;

(c) line printer with a printing speed of 300 lines a minute;

(d) four tape decks with a data transfer speed of 60 K b.p.s. (bytes per second);

(e) two disc drives each with a capacity of eight megabytes.

5. Considerations of proposed system. You are required to design a computerised system for the requirements outlined above showing the details outlined below:

(a) block diagram outlining the basic features of the system;

(b) system flowchart indicating where the computer fits into the proposed system;

(c) computer run chart showing the sequence and frequency of computer operations;

(d) layout of stock master file clearly indicating the data elements contained in stock records;

(e) punched card layouts in respect of stock transactions—G.R.N.s and issue notes;

(f) report layouts:
   (i) raw material stock schedule;
   (ii) raw material product analysis;

(g) an indication of essential checks and controls to be incorporated in the system;

(h) a design of a suitable coding system for raw materials and products including check digits;

(i) a formulation of appropriate assumptions (merely for exercise purposes) regarding the number and type of characters to assign to data elements particularly with regard to input cards and master file records.

The proposed system must be designed within the constraints of the existing configuration.

PREPARATION OF BLOCK DIAGRAM
AND SYSTEM FLOWCHART

6. Block diagram. Having studied the details of the current system and the requirements of any proposed system the first step is to prepare a simple diagram showing the outline of the system. The outline diagram is referred to as a block diagram or "system function" diagram (*see* Fig. 1). The purpose of the diagram is to provide a pictorial representation of the system showing inputs, files, processing and outputs, independent of operation details or the method to be used.

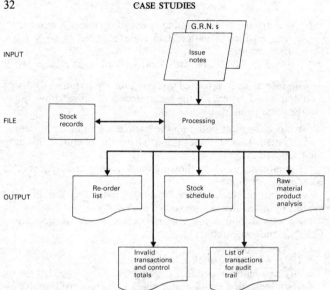

INPUT

FILE

OUTPUT

FIG. 1 *Block diagram: raw material stock and cost control.*

In this instance, although the proposed system is to be designed within the constraints of the existing computer configuration the block diagram does not show the computer. The diagram is mainly required to show the flow of information through the system.

7. System flowchart. This chart is prepared from the block diagram and, for the purpose of expanding the details, is shown by indicating where the computer fits into the system. The use to be made of the computer is indicated in broad terms, i.e. value transactions, update file and print reports. The flowchart also indicates that source documents (G.R.N.s and issue notes) are to be punched into cards for producing a transaction file for input to the computer in machine sensible characters. The distribution of the various print-outs is also shown (*see* Fig. 2).

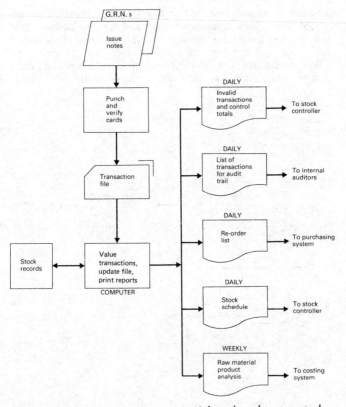

FIG. 2   *System flowchart: raw material stock and cost control.*

DESCRIPTION OF COMPUTER RUNS

8. General considerations. Referring to the computer run chart (*see* Fig. 3), it will be noticed that disc files are used throughout processing. To some extent this was determined on the basis of the file activity ratio which is stated in the terms of the case study to be, on average, 1:3. This particularly applies to run 4 which deals with updating the stock file, because processing time is saved compared with the situation where a tape is used because of the direct access nature of discs. Only those records currently affected by transactions need to be accessed whereas all records would have to be accessed on magnetic tape to update those affected by transactions. Further, a completely new stock master file would have to be rewritten if it was recorded on tape.

Magnetic tape could have been used in other processing runs if desired particularly as they are cheaper than disc packs.

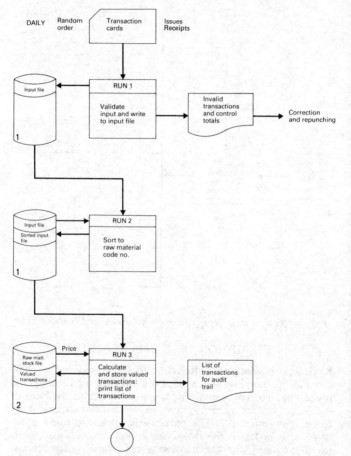

FIG. 3   *Computer run chart: raw material stock and cost control.*

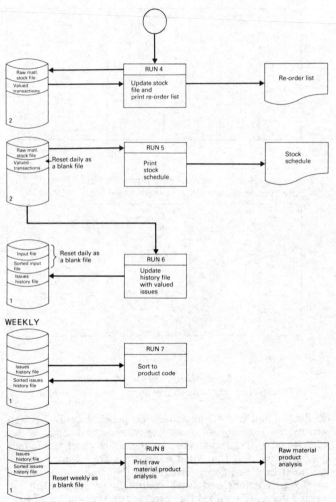

FIG. 3—contd.

However, it was considered that as it was only necessary to load two disc drives, instead of four tape decks on some occasions, handling time by the computer operator would be reduced.

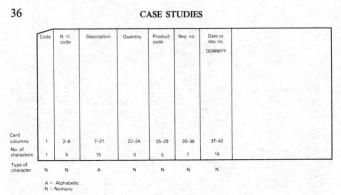

Card columns	1	2–6	7–21	22–24	25–29	30–36	37–42	
No. of characters	1	5	15	3	5	7	*6	
Type of character	N	N	A	N	N	N	N	

A = Alphabetic
N = Numeric

FIG. 4   *Punched card layout: issues.*

* Three numeric characters if day number used instead of date.

Card columns	1	2–6	7–21	22–24	25–31	32–37	
No. of characters	1	5	15	3	7	*6	
Type of character	N	N	A	N	N	N	

A = Alphabetic
N = Numeric

FIG. 5   *Punched card layout: receipts.*

* Three numeric characters if day number used instead of date.

9. Run 1. Batches of transactions on punched cards—receipts and issues—are input for processing each day and validated (*see* Figs. 4 and 5). The transactions are in random order and require sorting in the next run. Valid transactions are recorded on disc file no. 1 in a partition referred to as the input file. Details of invalid transactions and batch control totals are printed out. Invalid items are returned for correction and re-punching before being re-presented for processing. In this instance, the run can be stopped until all corrections are received, or processing may continue with the valid transactions. The corrected invalid transactions may then be processed the day they become available.

10. Run 2. The valid transactions in random order on disc file no. 1 are input for sorting into raw material code number sequence. This is to enable data to be accessed on a cylinder basis to minimise the time spent in searching for records during file updating. The cylinder mode of storing records requires sequential records to be stored on the same track on different disc surfaces in the disc pack. Time is saved by not having to move the read/write heads so frequently; they need only be moved to access a different cylinder of records, not individual records. The sorted transactions are recorded on disc file no. 1 in a partition referred to as the sorted input file.

11. Run 3. The sorted transactions from disc file no. 1 are input and the appropriate records stored on the raw material stock file, disc file no. 2, are accessed to obtain the price of the relevant raw material for calculating the value of each transaction. Valued transactions are then written to another partition of disc file no. 2. A print-out of the valued transactions is produced each day for the provision of an audit trail. This enables transactions to be traced through the various processing stages from the original source documents (issue notes and G.R.N.s) to punched cards and the printed list of transactions.

12. Run 4. The valued transactions are transferred from disc file no. 2 to the processor together with the relevant raw material records from a different partition of the same disc file. The appropriate records are then updated with the current transactions and written back to the same locations on the same disc file. As the raw material stock records contain the re-order level for each raw material it is compared with the revised stock quantity after applying current receipts and issues. If the quantity in stock is equal to, or less than, the re-order level then the item code is printed on a re-order list. As the code of the supplier and the Economic Order Quantity (E.O.Q.) are also recorded on the raw material records they are also printed on the re-order list. This is then dispatched to the purchasing department for the replenishment of supplies. *See* Figs. 6 and 7 for details of the raw material stock file.

13. Run 5. Stock records are read into the processor from the raw material stock file, recorded on disc file no. 2, for the purpose of printing a stock schedule showing current quantities and

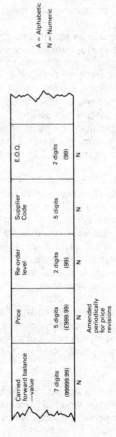

FIG. 6 *Layout of records on raw material stock file.*

FILE RECORD DEFINITION

File name: Raw Material Stock file

Type of file: Disc

Prepared by:

Date

Field No.	Name of field	A/N	Field length	Decimal point
1	Raw material code number (including check digit)	N	5	–
2	Description	A	15	–
3	B/F Bal.—quantity (tonnes)	N	2	1
4	B/F Bal.—value (£)	N	5	2
5	Daily receipts—quantity (tonnes)	N	2	1
6	Daily receipts—value (£)	N	5	2
7	Daily issues—quantity (tonnes)	N	2	1
8	Daily issues—value (£)	N	5	2
9	C/F Bal.—quantity (tonnes)	N	2	1
10	C/F Bal.—value (£)	N	5	2
11	Price (£)	N	3	2
12	Re-order level (tonnes)	N	2	–
13	Supplier code	N	5	–
14	E.O.Q. (tonnes)	N	2	–

A = Alphabetic
N = Numeric

FIG. 7 *Content of records on raw material stock file.*

RAW MATERIAL STOCK SCHEDULE

DATE:

STOCK NO.	STOCK DESCRIPTION	BROUGHT FORWARD BALANCE		RECEIPTS		ISSUES		CARRIED FORWARD BALANCE	
		QUANTITY	VALUE	QUANTITY	VALUE	QUANTITY	VALUE	QUANTITY	VALUE

FIG. 8 *Report layout: raw material stock schedule.*

values of raw materials in stock. The day's stock movements are also printed (*see* Fig. 8).

14. Run 6. The issues from the valued transactions file are input from disc file no. 2 each day and recorded on an issues history file on disc file no. 1. The file is updated each day of the current week.

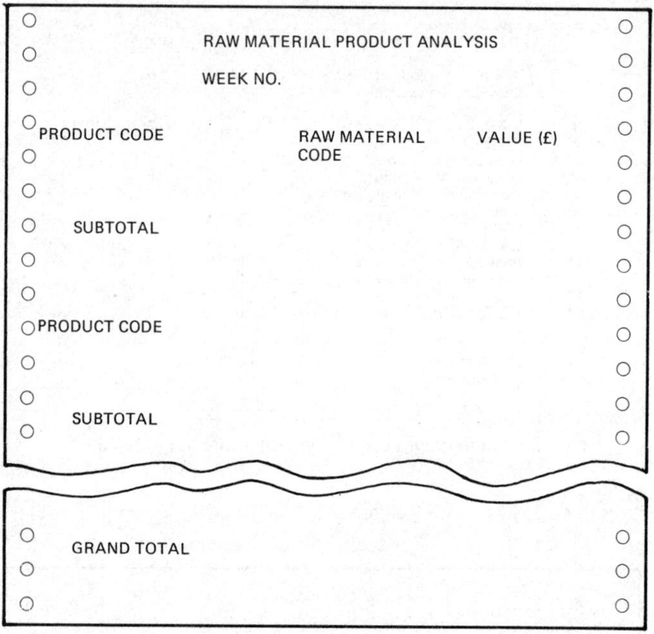

FIG. 9   *Report layout: raw material product analysis.*

15. Run 7. At the end of the week the issues history file is input to the computer from disc file no. 1. The issues are then sorted to product code and recorded on a different partition of disc file no. 1.

16. Run 8. The sorted issues history file is input from disc file no. 1 and the raw material product analysis is printed (*see* Fig. 9).

17. Observations. The valued transactions partition of disc file no. 2 is reset at the end of each day's processing as a blank file in readiness for the next day's run. The transactions are only stored temporarily as they are to be used in a later stage of processing.

Similarly, the input file and sorted input file partitions of disc file no. 1 are reset at the end of each day's processing as a blank file. The reason for this is that they are working file requirements for a specific day's processing only.

The issues history file and sorted issues history file partitions on disc file no. 1 are reset at the end of the week's processing as blank files having served the purpose of providing the details for printing a weekly raw material product analysis (*see* Fig. 9).

The only file remaining at the end of each week which is in the nature of a master file is the raw material stock file on disc file no. 2. This is because the quantity and value of materials in stock need to be carried forward to the next week.

18. File dumping. Although the run chart (*see* Fig. 3) does not indicate the situation, raw material records would need to be dumped after updating either to magnetic tape, another disc file or a different partition of the same disc file, for file security. If during the next run the raw material stock file was corrupted or erased in error, then it would be possible to reconstitute the file from the security copy.

CHECKS AND CONTROLS

19. Checks and controls—general considerations. A number of checks and controls may be applied to the data relating to the raw material stock control and cost control system. It is of course essential to ensure data is for the correct period before processing commences, that is the correct day in respect of stock movements. It is also necessary to ensure that data is of the correct type, that is stock data rather than payroll data or sales data, etc. Other checks and controls include checks to ensure that the correct disc file is being used. Specific checks and controls to be outlined include validity checks by means of check digit verification to ensure the accuracy of raw material and product code numbers, batch controls, audit controls, limit checks and field checks.

20. Check digit verification (validity check). Check digits are generally used for the purpose of ensuring that identification fields in transaction data are valid (*see* Table IV). A number of methods may be adopted two of which are demonstrated below in respect of raw material and product code numbers. It is first necessary to list the relevant range of numbers which we may assume has already been established (*see* Tables V and VI).

TABLE V. SCHEDULE OF RAW MATERIAL CODE NUMBERS

Material	Code
Steel rod	0001–0170
Steel strip	0171–0340
Steel sheet	0341–0500
Copper rod	0550–0670
Copper strip	0671–0840
Copper sheet	0841–1000
Brass rod	1050–1200
Brass strip	1201–1400
Brass sheet	1401–1550
Electric cable	1600–1850

TABLE VI. SCHEDULE OF PRODUCT CODE NUMBERS

Product	Code
Kettles	3000–3500
Irons	4000–4500
Fires	5000–5500

21. Calculation of check digit for raw material code numbers. A simple method which may be applied is to obtain the "sum of the digits" of a specific code number to derive a single digit to be used as a check digit. An example will assist in clarifying the use of the method. Referring to the schedule of raw material code numbers (*see* Table V), let it be assumed that a check digit is required for brass sheet, code number 1549. It may be calculated as follows:

(*a*) $1 + 5 + 4 + 9 = 19$ (sum of digits);

(*b*) to obtain a single check digit it is necessary to add again: $1 + 9 = 10$;

(*c*) the above stage must be repeated; $1 + 0 = 1$. The check digit to be added to the code number is 1 and the number becomes 15491.

22. Calculation of check digit for product code numbers. The same method as outlined above may be used, but for the purpose of widening the reader's knowledge of the use of check digits a different method will be demonstrated. The method to be used is calculated in the following way:

(*a*) add even numbered digits;

(*b*) add odd numbered digits;

(*c*) multiply the results of (*a*) and (*b*);

(*d*) add the digits in (*c*) if there are two or more.

Referring to the schedule of product code numbers (*see* Table VI), it may be assumed that a check digit is required for electric iron, product number 4136. It may be calculated as follows:

(*a*) $4 + 6 = 10$;

(*b*) $1 + 3 = 4$;

(*c*) $10 \times 4 = 40$;

(*d*) $4 + 0 = 4$. The check digit to be added to the code number is 4 and the number becomes 41364.

23. Batch controls. Control of batches of input data ensures that not only are all transactions processed but that they are processed correctly. For this purpose batch control totals are calculated which may consist of the number of documents in a batch for making sure that all transactions have been accounted for. Other control totals may consist of quantities and values of the different transaction types contained in particular batches in respect of receipts into store and issues from store. A "Hash" total of the different stock numbers of items in a batch may also be applied. Such totals, whatever form they may take, are recorded on a batch control slip. The totals are input with the data for processing and the computer generates similar totals during the processing of batches of transactions. Any difference from the batch control totals pre-listed and those generated by the computer are reported by being printed out so that they may be investigated and appropriate corrections effected (*see* Fig. 3, run 1).

24. Audit controls. For the purpose of monitoring the performance and accuracy of data processing operations auditors are often supplied with a print-out of transactions processed and updated on the master file during a specific period, thereby providing an audit trail. By this means the auditors can ensure that all source documents for a period have been dealt with by making sure that they agree with those listed on the print-out (*see* Fig. 3, run 3).

25. Limit check. This check may be applied to issues of raw materials to detect any quantities which have exceeded normal levels. Abnormalities can then be subjected to further checks to verify whether the data contains errors. This prevents stock records showing a false situation and also ensures that products are correctly charged (*see* Fig. 7, field no. 7).

26. Field checks. Referring to Figs. 4 and 5 it can be seen that each field has the number and type of character specified. This detail is contained in the computer program which enables the computer to check each field as it is input. Any field which differs regarding the number or type of character it contains to that specified is rejected. This is how invalid data is detected and prevented from being processed. Invalid transactions must be corrected and re-presented for processing.

OVERVIEW OF CASE STUDY I

This is to enable the reader to check what has been learnt of systems design from this case study and as a basis for review:

(*a*) purpose and manner of constructing various types of diagram and charts to indicate various features of systems, in this instance, block diagram, system flowchart and computer run chart;

(*b*) the logical sequence of computer processing operations to achieve a defined purpose as depicted on a computer run chart;

(*c*) the mode of constructing data fields on punched cards for the provision of input to the computer;

(*d*) the layout of fields for the construction of records on a magnetic type master file;

(*e*) the manner of preparing a file record definition;

(*f*) the manner of preparing report layouts (horizontal and vertical spacing requirements not specified);

(g) reason for, and the type of, checks and controls which may be incorporated in a system including the manner of calculating check digits;

(h) the reason for incorporating audit trails within systems.

CASE STUDIES II AND III

Structural and Fabricated Engineering: Payroll and Labour Costing

GENERAL CONSIDERATIONS

1. Company profile. J. S. Forster & Co. Limited offers comprehensive services in respect of all types of structural and fabricated engineering projects. Activities range from small, "fabricate only" jobs to survey, design, detail, fabricate and erection of complete plant installations. Fifty per cent of the company's production is, directly or indirectly, for export markets. Fabrications are produced for mechanical handling, the processing industries, foundries, etc., and include pressure vessels, boilers, chimneys, cupolas, heat-exchangers, conveyors, waggon-tipplers, crane-girders, etc.

The company's 30,000 m² site includes six main bays with specialist fabrication areas. These are equipped with comprehensive cranage and facilities for sawing, punching, cropping, drilling, welding, flame-cutting, shearing, plate edge-planing, girder end-milling, bending, folding and rolling. A large stock-yard contains an extensive range of steel plate and sections and there is indoor and outdoor storage available for finished fabrications. Stress-relieving, non-destructive testing, shot-blasting and paint spraying are carried out by specialist sub-contractors on and off the premises.

2. Adequacy of existing method. In 1974 the company applied for an extension of a maintenance agreement for the Remington Soemtron Miniputer which had been in use for nine years. The company was informed that the machine was obsolete and that spares would not be available except by cannibalisation of trade-in machines.

Frequent stoppages were experienced and the engineers called in were sceptical of their ability to maintain the machine. The machine cost £4,000 and was purchased for the processing of labour costing, payroll, sales ledger and purchase ledger.

However, the machine never handled the labour costing application satisfactorily and no other application was implemented owing to initial troubles causing tedious off-line operations. No facility was available to store and carry forward some 200 contract balances spread over twelve heads of operations analysis. This has been done manually for nearly ten years. It has been necessary to pre-sort all input data into strict contract and operations sequence by use of paper slips—again manually. This method takes approximately one and a half man-days per week. A further one and a half man-days is taken up by data input and review print-out. Balancing back to the payroll requires a further half-day to perform manually, assuming there are no problems. The average time taken to process the whole of the labour costing system is four days per week.

3. Investigations. The Board authorised a search for an up-to-date replacement of the existing machine and, accordingly, many exhibitions, seminars and demonstrations were attended. The company secretary familiarised himself with nine makes of machines ranging from electronic accounting machines to sophisticated disc based computers. It was found that between £5,000 and £8,000 no suitable machine was available. In the upper range there was a choice of Visible Record Computers consisting of magnetic ledger machines, machines using ordinary ledger cards and those using magnetic cassettes costing between £8,000 and £15,000.

Two machines in particular appeared to be suitable for the company's system requirements, the Kienzle 6000 and the N.C.R. 399. From private demonstrations by both companies it became clear that the company's particular needs would best be served by the N.C.R. 399 because of its facility for capturing data on magnetic cassette together with a processor of adequate capacity.

Back-up service by N.C.R. Limited is generally acknowledged to be effective but the company secretary reported to the Board at the beginning of 1975 that he could not recommend the level of expenditure necessary for implementation of the N.C.R. 399 due to the economic climate prevailing at the time. He suggested the alternative recently marketed N.C.R. 299 costing £6,000. The Board, however, made the decision to acquire the N.C.R. 399 at a hardware cost in the region of £12,000 with additional costs of approximately £6,000 covering programming, installation and staff training.

The reader must appreciate that the costs quoted were relevant at the time and have been included for comparative purpose rather than as a guide to present costs.

4. Specification of N.C.R. 399. A brief outline of the machine's basic features follows.

(*a*) Third generation processor with an internal memory capacity of 16 K bytes.

(*b*) Three cassette stations with the ability to sort, merge, extract, print-out, program and store.

(*c*) Machine command keyboard.

(*d*) Alpha/numeric input keyboard.

(*e*) Communication indicators to operator.

(*f*) Continuous forms feeder.

(*g*) Automatic line find for use with plain ledger cards.

5. Hardware obsolescence. It is important for the reader to appreciate that the N.C.R. 399 is not a current model but is currently in use at J. S. Forster & Co. Ltd. The current range of information processing systems from N.C.R. is the 8000 series which incorporates larger memories, disc storage facilities, visual display unit and visual record printer or line printer, etc. The specific features depend upon the particular model.

The reader must also appreciate that the data processing field is changing at a faster rate than ever, due to advances in computer technology. Businesses, however, cannot constantly upgrade their system's hardware in an attempt to harness the latest technology, due to considerations of cost and disruption of current systems. Even though hardware may become technologically obsolete it may still have a useful system's life and perform economically as far as a specific business is concerned.

It is also important for the reader to be aware that the approach to designing a system for implementation on a V.R.C., rather than a main frame computer, is the same; this is the primary purpose of including Case Studies II and III in this book.

6. Hourly paid and weekly salaries payrolls. Two payrolls are produced each week, one for hourly paid employees and one for weekly salaries. The same suite of programs provides for the processing needs of both payrolls. Each payroll is prepared by separate runs.

Hourly Paid Payroll

GENERAL CONSIDERATIONS

7. Introduction. Before studying the details of this case study, the reader is recommended to pause a while to consider the essential elements of a payroll system for hourly paid employees (including piecework) in order to have some basis with which to compare the details which follow. In this way it is hoped that the reader will assist the learning process by discovering what was already known and what has been learnt after studying the case study.

Considerations should include:

(*a*) definition of payroll master file, clearly indicating the data elements it should contain in respect of employee payroll details;

(*b*) method of creating the initial payroll master file and the procedure for dealing with file amendments;

(*c*) input specification;

(*d*) other types of file required in the system either for updating or for reference purposes;

(*e*) basis of calculating National Insurance contributions, net pay, holiday credits, sickness holiday credit and the structure of taxable gross pay for the week, etc.;

(*f*) preparation prior to processing;

(*g*) operator input;

(*h*) machine processing operations;

(*i*) output specification.

8. Objectives of hourly paid payroll. To accept hours and piecework input and to refer to internally stored daywork rates and tax factors, etc. for the purpose of calculating gross pay, P.A.Y.E., holiday credits and National Insurance contributions; and to prepare a summary of these figures together with a note and coin analysis and duplicated payslips, etc. Also to provide accumulated figures to date for each employee in respect of gross pay, tax, National Insurance, accrued holiday credits, employer's share of National Insurance, etc. In addition to print out automatically an annual return relating to P.A.Y.E. and National Insurance at the end of the year.

9. Structure of the system. The weekly hourly paid payroll application has the following main sections.

(a) Creation of payroll master file.

(b) Amendments to payroll master file.

(c) Creation of tax and National Insurance factors file.

(d) Hourly payroll weekly processing rouutine:
   (i) preparation for processing;
   (ii) operator input;
   (iii) machine operations;
   (iv) input proof sheet;
   (v) pay advice slip;
   (vi) payroll totals;
   (vii) note and coin analysis.

(e) General system requirements.

(f) Input proof sheet error corrections.

The main features of the weekly processing routine are outlined on the system flowchart (*see* Fig. 10). The processing routine is also outlined below which may be studied in conjunction with the flowchart.

10. Elements of the system. The basic elements of the payroll system may be analysed as follows.

(a) Input—Payroll weekly input data sheet (*see* Fig. 13).

(b) Processing (*see* **14–16**).

(c) Storage—files used in the system:
   (i) daywork rates file (*see* Fig. 19);
   (ii) tax and National Insurance factors;
   (iii) brought forward payroll master file (*see* Fig. 12);
   (iv) carried forward payroll master file (*see* Fig. 12);
   (v) security copy of (IV).

(d) Output:
   (i) input proof sheet (*see* Fig. 14);
   (ii) pay advice slip (*see* Fig. 15);
   (iii) payroll totals—summary pay advice slip;
   (iv) note and coin analysis;
   (v) annual return of P.A.Y.E. and National Insurance.

11. Creation of payroll master file. The file creation document is shown in Fig. 11 and it is used by the operator for entering data through the keyboard of the 399 in respect of employee details which are stored on a magnetic cassette.

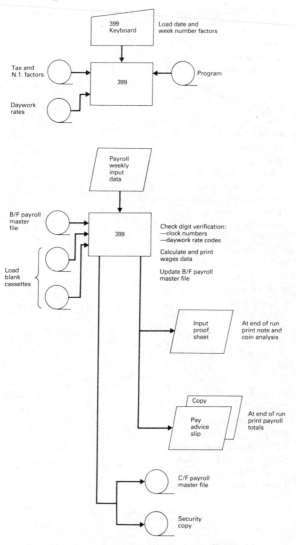

FIG. 10 *System flowchart: hourly paid payroll.*

J. S. FORSTER — PAYROLL   FILE/CREATION & AMENDMENT
                            DOCUMENT

```
 1 Name                    └─┴─┴─┴─┴─┴─┴─┴─┴─┴─┴─┴─┴─┴─┴─┴─┴─┴─┘
 2 Tax code prefix         └─┘  ⎫
 3 Tax code suffix         └─┘  ⎬ Alternatives
 4 N. I. No.               └─┴─┴─┴─┴─┴─┴─┴─┘
 5 N. I. category          └─┘
 6 Clock No.                                    └─┴─┴─┴─▨▨▨
 7 Tax code    Numeric portion only             └─┴─┴─▨▨▨▨
 8 Week 1 indicator                             └─▨▨▨▨
 9 Daywork to date                              └─┴─┴─┴─┴─┴─┘
10 Piecework to date                            └─┴─┴─┴─┴─┴─┘
11 Overtime prem. to date                       └─┴─┴─┴─┴─┴─┘
12 Holiday credit to date                       └─┴─┴─┴─┴─▨▨
13 Sick hol. credit weeks to date               └─┴─┴─▨▨▨▨
14 Taxable gross to date                        └─┴─┴─┴─┴─┴─┘
15 Tax to date                                  └─┴─┴─┴─┴─┴─┘
16 Basic N. I. code   A   to date               └─┴─┴─┴─┴─┴─┘
17 Total N. I. code   A   to date               └─┴─┴─┴─┴─┴─┘
18 Basic N. I. code   B   to date               └─┴─┴─┴─┴─┴─┘
19 Total N. I. code   B   to date               └─┴─┴─┴─┴─┴─┘
20 Basic N. I. code   C   to date               └─┴─┴─┴─┴─┴─┘
21 Total N. I. code   C   to date               └─┴─┴─┴─┴─┴─┘
22 Fixed deds    1    S & D                      └─┴─┴─┴─┘
23               2    charities                  └─┴─┴─┴─┘
24               3    over-alls                  └─┴─┴─┴─┘
25               4                               └─┴─┴─┴─┘
26               5                               └─┴─┴─┴─┘
27               6                               └─┴─┴─┴─┘
28               7                               └─┴─┴─┴─┘
29               8                               └─┴─┴─┴─┘
30 Weekly salary amount                         └─┴─┴─┴─┴─┘
31 Holiday credit flat rate                      └─┴─┴─┴─┘
32 Gross in previous employment                 └─┴─┴─┴─┴─┴─┘
33 Tax in previous employment                   └─┴─┴─┴─┴─┴─┘
34 Week 53 gross                                └─┴─┴─┴─┴─┘
35 Week 53 tax                                  └─┴─┴─┴─┴─┘

                          HASH TOTAL            └─┴─┴─┴─┴─┴─┘
```

FIG. 11   *File creation and amendment document.*

FILE RECORD DEFINITION

Storage media: Cassette

Application: Weekly hourly paid payroll and weekly salaries

File name: Payroll master file

Prepared by:

Date prepared:

Field No.	Name of field	X/N	Field length	Decimal places
1	Clock No.	N	3	–
2	Name	X	20	–
3	Tax code prefix } alternatives	X	1	–
4	Tax code suffix	X	1	–
5	Tax code	N	3	–
6	National Insurance No.	X/N	9	–
7	National Insurance Category	X	1	–
8	Daywork to date	N	4	2
9	Piecework to date	N	4	2
10	Overtime premium to date	N	4	2
11	Holiday credit to date	N	4	2
12	Sickness holiday credit weeks to date	N	2	–
13	Taxable gross to date	N	4	2
14	Tax to date	N	4	2
15	Employee's N. I. to date	N	3	2
16	Total N. I. contributions to date	N	3	2
17	Fixed deductions:			
	1. S & D	N	1	2
	2. Charities (Char)	N	1	2
	3. Over–alls (Overs)	N	1	2
	4. Blank	N	1	2
	5. „	N	1	2
	6. „	N	1	2
	7. „	N	1	2
	8. „	N	1	2
18	Taxable gross earnings previous employment	N	4	2
19	Tax previous employment	N	4	2
20	Weekly salary amount	N	3	2
21	Holiday credit flat rate	N	2	2

X = Alphabetic character
N = Numeric character

FIG. 12 *File record definition: payroll master file.*

(a) The employee's tax code normally takes the form 999X (e.g. 33ØH) but on occasions the tax code may take the form of 999XX (e.g. 191HO) as shown on the pay advice slip (*see* Fig. 15). The O indicates that the code is not a week 1 basis when there has been an adjustment to an employee's tax allowance. (b) National insurance numbers are a combination of both alphabetic and numeric characters, i.e. two alpha, six numeric and one alpha. An actual example is AB39256ØB as shown on the pay advice slip.

12. Amendments to payroll master file. Single fields can be amended and new employees added but leavers will not be removed from the file until the start of a new tax year. This enables any year-end tax routines to be automatic. This procedure necessitates the allocation of clock numbers to new employees which have not previously been issued in the same tax year. The same document is used for amendments as for initial file creation (*see* Fig. 11).

13. Payroll master file definition. Details of the master file are shown in Fig. 12. The file is updated each week as part of the payroll processing routine. The file definition clearly shows the number and type of character in each field. The reader may be surprised at the number of details (data elements) contained in an employee record. A security copy is obtained each time the file is updated as a precaution against the possible loss of records on the normal file. The security copy means that the system can continue as important records are not lost as would be the case if the records on the normal file were accidentally erased or overwritten.

HOURLY PAYROLL WEEKLY PROCESSING ROUTINE

14. Preparation for processing. The machine operator attends to the following requirements (*see* Fig. 10).

(*a*) Selection and loading of program.

(*b*) Loading of date and week number factors through the keyboard.

(*c*) Loading of tax, N.I. factors and daywork rates into memory from cassettes and then removal of cassettes from cassette stations.

(*d*) Loading of two cassette stations with blank cassettes for capturing updated employee records and obtaining a security copy.

(*e*) Loading of input proof sheet and two-part pay advice stationery.

15. Operator input. From the batch of payroll weekly input data sheets (prepared from clock cards and piecework sheets, *see* Fig. 13), the operator enters pay and other details via the 399 keyboard. When clock numbers and daywork rate codes are entered

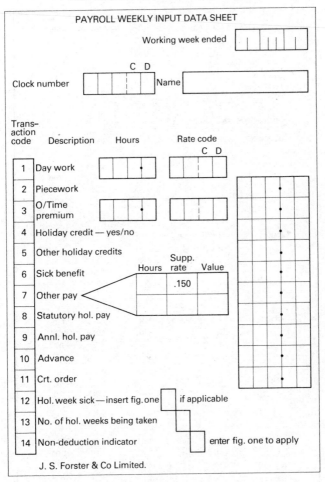

FIG. 13 *Payroll weekly input data sheet.*

they are automatically subjected to check digit verification by the program. The clock numbers and associated check digits are identical to those used for the labour costing application. Input is

INPUT PROOF SHEET

J.S. FORSTER & CO. LTD.   WAGES & SALARIES

DATE	31MAR79				
WEEK NO.	52				
RUN TYPE	1				
RATES OK					
LOAD OK					
000					

HD0399   MSTER   290378   51

CLOCK NO	CODE	HOURS	RATE CODE	RATE	AMOUNT
XXXX1	1	60.4	1911	1.173	70.85
	2				2.00
	3	26.4	3108	.893	23.58
	4				4.18
	7				7.08
XXXX2	1	32.5	1911	1.173	38.12
	2				2.00
	3	.2	3108	.893	.18
	4	(SICK)			4.18
	7				3.81
	9				10.03
XXXX3	1	43.5	1203	1.316	57.25
	3	1.9	2406	1.050	2.00
	4				4.90
	7				5.72
XXXX4	1	21.5	1911	1.173	25.22
	3	2.0	3108	.893	1.79
	4				2.24
	7				2.52
XXXX5	1	51.8	1911	1.173	60.76
	2				2.00
	3	7.6	3108	.893	6.79
	4				4.18
	7				6.08
	11				1.13

FIG. 14   *Input proof sheet.*

required in strict clock number sequence for the payroll routine because the master file is in clock number sequence.

16. Machine operations. Having set up the job and entered the relevant payroll data the machine automatically performs the following operations under control of the stored program (*see* Fig. 10).

(*a*) Check digit verification of clock numbers and daywork rate codes.

(*b*) Calculate and print wages data on input sheet and duplicate pay advice slip.

(*c*) Update B/F payroll master file in memory and record updated file on two blank cassettes, one of which is the C/F payroll master file and the other a security copy.

(*d*) Print payroll totals and note and coin analysis.

17. Input proof sheet. The purpose of the proof sheet is to ensure that all input from payroll weekly input data sheets in respect of each employee is input accurately. The data printed on the input proof sheet is that entered by the operator. By reference to Figs. 13 and 14 it will be observed that the transaction codes correspond. The basic data printed on the input proof sheet includes:

(*a*) clock no. including check digit;
(*b*) transaction code;
(*c*) daywork hours;
(*d*) rate code;
(*e*) piecework amount;
(*f*) overtime premium hours and rate code;
(*g*) other entries as appropriate.

The clock numbers shown on Fig. 14 are fictitious for reasons of confidentiality and the daywork rates and overtime premium rates are obtained from the daywork rates file.

18. Pay advice slip. The basic data printed on the pay advice slip (*see* Fig. 15), is identical to that printed on the input proof sheet and is obtained from payroll weekly input data sheets. The specification of pay advice slip data fields and the source of specific entries are portrayed in Table VII (*see* Fig. 12 for references to master file).

PAY ADVICE

	HOURS	RATE	AMOUNT THIS WEEK	AMOUNT Y.T.D.
DAYWORK/ SALARY	51.8	1.173	60.76	2,906.81
PIECEWORK/BONUS			2.00	143.50
O/T. PREMIUM	7.6	.893	6.79	788.53
HOL. CREDIT			4.18	150.46
SICKNESS BEN.			.00	–
OTHER PAY			6.08	–
STAT. HOL. PAY			.00	–
TAXABLE GROSS			79.81	4,558.05
ANN. HOL. PAY			.00	
INCOME TAX			14.60	896.20
EMPLOYEE N.I.			4.35	239.98
FIXED DEDS.			.09	
ADV. OF WAGES			.00	
COURT ORDERS			1.13	
HOL. CRED.			4.18CR	
NET PAY			55.46	

S & D	CHAR	OVERS					
.07	.02	.00	.00	.00	.00	.00	.00

WEEK No.	52
INCOME TAX CODE	191HO
N.I. CODE	AB392560B
N.I. CATEGORY	A
TOTAL CONTRIB. TO DATE	688.67
GROSS FOR WEEK FOR N.I.	75.63
SICKNESS HOL. CRED. WEEKS	
CLOCK No.	XX5
DATE	31MAR79
NAME	A B CHESTER
NET PAY	55.46

FIG. 15 *Pay advice slip.*

TABLE VII. SPECIFICATION OF DATA FIELDS AND SOURCE OF ENTRIES ON PAY ADVICE SLIP

Source of entry	*Field length*	
Daywork/salary:		
Hours (entered by operator)	999.9	
Rate code (entered but not printed)	99.99	Includes two check digits
Rate (from daywork rates file)	9.999	

TABLE VII.—*contd.*

Source of entry	Field length	
Amount this week (calculated)	999.99	
Amount Y.T.D. (derived from updated master file)	9999.99	
Piecework/bonus:		
Amount this week (entry of predetermined amount)	999.99	
Amount Y.T.D. (derived from updated master file)	9999.99	
Overtime premium:		
Hours	999.9	
Rate (from daywork rates file)	9.999	
Rate code (entered but not printed)	99.99	Includes two check digits
Amount this week (calculated)	999.99	
Amount Y.T.D. (derived from updated master file)	9999.99	
Holiday credit:		
Amount this week (flat rate from master file or calculated)	999.99	
Amount Y.T.D. (derived from updated master file)	9999.99	
Sickness benefit (applicable to weekly salaries):		
Amount this week (as applicable)	999.99	

TABLE VII.—*contd.*

Source of entry	Field length
Other pay:	
Amount this week (as applicable)	999.99
Statutory holiday pay:	
Amount this week (as applicable)	999.99
Taxable gross:	
Amount this week (calculated)	999.99
Amount Y.T.D. (derived from updated master file)	9999.99 9999.99
Annual holiday pay:	
Amount this week (as applicable)	
Income tax:	
Amount this week (calculated)	999.99
Amount Y.T.D. (derived from updated master file)	9999.99
Employee N.I.:	
Amount this week (calculated)	999.99
Amount Y.T.D. (derived from updated master file)	999.99
Fixed deductions:	
Amount this week (derived from master file)	9.99

TABLE VII.—*contd.*

Source of entry	Field length
Advance of wages:	
Amount this week (as applicable)	999.99
Court orders:	
Amount this week (as applicable)	999.99
Holiday credit (other holiday credit):	
Amount this week (entry of predetermined amount)	999.99
Net pay:	
Amount this week (calculated)	999.99
Week Number:	
Entered by operator at beginning of run	99
Income tax code:	
Derived from master file	
National Insurance Number (code):	
Derived from mmster file	
National Insurance category:	
Derived from master file	IX

TABLE VII.—*contd.*

Source of entry	Field length	
Total Contributions to date (N.I.):		
Derived from updated master file	999.99	
Gross for week for National Insurance: Calculated, *see* **30**	999.99	
Sickness holiday credit weeks:		
The digit I is entered each week as appropriate up to a maximum of twelve weeks, *see* **26**	99	
Clock number:		
Entered by operator	999.99	Includes two check digits
Date (working week ended):		
Entered by operator at beginning of run	DDMMM YY I.E. 31 MAR 78	
Name:		
Automatically printed from master file		
Net pay:		
Repeat printed	999.99	

PAYROLL TOTALS AND
NOTE AND COIN ANALYSIS

19. Payroll totals. The following totals are produced and printed on a pay advice slip after completion of all employees' pay calculations:

(*a*) daywork hours and value;
(*b*) piecework value;
(*c*) overtime premium hours and value;
(*d*) holiday credit;
(*e*) sickness benefit (*see* weekly salaries, p.68);
(*f*) other pay;
(*g*) statutory holiday pay;
(*h*) taxable gross for week;
(*i*) annual holiday pay;
(*j*) income tax;
(*k*) employee's National Insurance;
(*l*) analysis of fixed deductions;
(*m*) advance of wages;
(*n*) court orders;
(*o*) other holiday credit;
(*p*) net pay;
(*q*) total contribution to National Insurance—employer;
(*r*) gross for week for National Insurance.

20. Note and coin analysis. In order to determine exact requirements from the bank for making up each employee's pay envelope a note and coin analysis is necessary for determining the number required of the following:

(*a*) £5 notes;
(*b*) £1 notes;
(*c*) 50 pence pieces;
(*d*) 10 pence pieces;
(*e*) 5 pence pieces;
(*f*) 2 pence pieces;
(*g*) 1 pence pieces.

The analysis is computed and accumulated when each employee's pay is calculated.

As the payroll is not sectionalised the above totals will only be required upon completion of the entire payroll. However, provision should be made to print the totals whenever required and to re-enter these totals manually before re-commencing the payroll run. This will cover the situation of a break in the payroll run being necessary for any reason. Provision should be made for printing a hash total of the totals printed so as to provide a means of automatically agreeing the manually re-entered totals with those generated by the program.

GENERAL SYSTEM REQUIREMENTS

21. Various requirements. These may be summarised as follows.

(a) An earnings and tax record card is not used as the relevant employee data is recorded on the payroll master file which is a magnetic cassette. This eliminates card selection and loading which saves time.

(b) Cumulative to-date information will be printed weekly on the duplicated pay advice slips.

(c) The pay advice slip must be designed so that the clock number and name of each employee is clearly visible in the window of the pay envelope.

(d) All variable information must first be printed on to an input proof sheet before being printed on to pay advice slips.

22. Daywork earnings. A number of important considerations include the following.

(a) Parts of an hour are expressed in units of six minutes therefore 1.1 = one hour and six minutes, and 1.2 = one hour and twelve minutes. Also refer to labour costing application.

(b) When calculating daywork earnings the daywork rate will be selected from memory by indexing the rate code (*see* **14**(*c*)).

(c) The daywork amount is to be rounded to the nearest whole penny; therefore round .4 of a penny down and .5 of a penny up.

23. Piecework. Important points to be aware of include the following.

(a) Piecework will always be an entry of a pre-determined amount (*see* **17**(*e*)).

(b) Piecework is not applicable to every employee.

(c) There is only one entry each week for each employee concerned in respect of piecework amount.

24. Overtime premium. Points for consideration include the following.

(*a*) Overtime is not applicable to every employee.

(*b*) Overtime hours will be entered from the payroll weekly input data sheets.

(*c*) Rate code will be entered by the operator from the payroll weekly input data sheets and the appropriate rate will be indexed from the internally stored daywork rates. Amounts will be calculated and rounded to the nearest whole penny as indicated in **22** (*c*) above.

(*d*) There could be up to two different rates per employee, one being applicable when working on-site and the other when in the works.

25. Holiday credit. Aspects to take into account include the following.

(*a*) It is not applicable to every employee, only hourly paid employees.

(*b*) A flat rate applies for a forty-hour week.

(*c*) The sum of the daywork hours entered from the payroll weekly input data sheets is compared with forty hours and if the daywork hours are greater than or equal to forty hours the flat rate will apply. If daywork hours are less than forty hours the calculation for holiday credit is as follows:

$$\frac{\text{daywork hours}}{40 \text{ hours}} \times \text{flat rate}$$

(*d*) In addition to the above calculation there could be a further holiday credit amount (other holiday credit) which will be entered as a pre-determined amount.

(*e*) The holiday credit amount (including other holiday credit) is taxed in the week in which the holiday credit is calculated. The holiday credit amount(s) is therefore included in gross pay for the week.

(*f*) The amount of the holiday credit (including other holiday credit) is deducted from gross pay after calculating tax.

(*g*) When paid out the annual holiday pay is not taxed.

(*h*) The holiday credit is deducted from gross pay for the purpose of calculating National Insurance as the Social Security Act 1973 requires that N.I. deductions be made at the time of payment.

26. Sickness holiday credit. The following considerations apply.

(*a*) The sickness holiday credit weeks represent the number of weeks that an employee has been sick in a year. It will always reflect whole weeks even though an employee may have been away for only part of one or more of the weeks. The holiday week sickness entered on the input proof sheet will be added to the sickness holiday credit weeks. The number to be entered on the I.P.S. will be decided by the operator who will make the appropriate entry, i.e. the digit 1 each week the employee is sick as an accumulation up to a maximum of twelve weeks.

(b) Holiday credit is applicable for twelve weeks' sickness in any year.

(c) An employee is only entitled to holiday credit if a sickness certificate is presented on time.

(d) The various combinations of calculating sickness holiday credit are as follows:

(i) full holiday credit flat rate if the certificate is presented on time irrespective of the daywork hours applicable;

(ii) $\dfrac{\text{daywork hours}}{40 \text{ hours}} \times$ flat rate (if certificate not presented on time);

(iii) no holiday credit if certificate not presented on time and the employee has not worked during the week;

(iv) no holiday credit beyond twelve weeks' sickness in any year.

27. Taxable gross pay for the week. This amount is the sum of the following:

(a) daywork;
(b) piecework;
(c) overtime premium;
(d) holiday credit;
(e) other holiday credit;
(f) other pay;
(g) statutory holiday pay.

Although a year-to-date total is printed it is not directly reconcilable by adding the above mentioned items on the pay advice slip because of the incidence of holiday payments.

28. Analysis of fixed deductions. Provision is made for eight deductions but only three have been allocated. The deductions when appropriate for a particular employee are printed automatically as they are stored on the payroll master file (*see* Fig. 12).

29. Income tax. This is a standard routine which includes provision not to pay a tax refund over the statutory maximum allowed for any new employee until authority is subsequently obtained.

30. Employee's National Insurance contribution. This is a standard routine and the contribution is calculated on the sum of the following items as a percentage:

(*a*) daywork amount;
(*b*) piecework amount;
(*c*) overtime premium amount;
(*d*) other pay;
(*e*) statutory holiday pay;
(*f*) annual holiday pay.

31. Net pay. This figure is calculated in the following way.

(*a*) Taxable gross pay for week including statutory holiday pay and annual holiday pay, minus:
(*b*) income tax;
(*c*) employee's N.I.;
(*d*) fixed deductions;
(*e*) advance of wages;
(*f*) court orders;
(*g*) holiday credit.

32. Other pay. Applies to extraordinary items, e.g. pay awards and pay arrears.

33. Statutory holiday pay. Payment for bank holidays.

34. Annual holiday pay. Payment of accrued holiday credits (*see* 25).

35. Advance of wages. A variable deduction which does not apply to every employee but is entered as a predetermined amount when applicable.

36. Court orders. Same considerations apply as indicated above.

INPUT PROOF SHEET ERROR CORRECTIONS

37. Notice before pay advice slip updated. Provision is made for rejecting entire records when input errors are detected and for re-entering corrected data.

38. Clock numbers out of sequence. Provision is also made for producing pay advice slips for clock numbers entered out of sequence as a separate run, at the end of the normal run.

WEEKLY SALARIES

As stated previously, the same program is used for preparing weekly salaries as is used for the hourly payroll, with the exception of the following items (*see* **39–42**).

39. Build-up to gross pay. The build-up is as follows.

(*a*) Gross pay is a fixed amount applied automatically from data encoded on the payroll master file.

(*b*) Bonus is a variable amount entered by the operator.

(*c*) Overtime is also a variable amount entered by the operator.

(*d*) Other pay is similarly a variable amount entered by the operator.

(*e*) Sickness benefit is a variable amount entered by the operator which is subtracted from other figures in arriving at taxable gross for the week.

40. Pay advice stationery. In order to use common pay advice slips for both types of payroll the following common headings are printed on the pay advice slips:

(*a*) daywork/salary (*see* Fig. 15);

(*b*) piecework/bonus;

(*c*) overtime;

(*d*) sickness benefit;

(*e*) other pay.

41. Number and types of character. The capacities applicable to the weekly hourly paid payroll also apply to the weekly salaries build-up to gross items.

42. Holiday credit. Holiday credits do not apply to weekly salaries; neither does holiday weeks' sickness.

OVERVIEW OF CASE STUDY II

This is to enable the reader to check what has been learnt of systems design from this case study and as a basis for review.

(*a*) Definition of the problem.

(*b*) The need to investigate alternative methods prior to selection of most suitable method.

(*c*) Specification of system objectives.

(*d*) Structure of an hourly paid payroll system.

(*e*) Creation of a master file on appropriate storage media.

(*f*) Payroll processing routine.

(*g*) General system requirements in respect of matters relating to:

  (*i*) daywork earnings;

  (*ii*) piecework;

  (*iii*) overtime premium;

  (*iv*) holiday credit;

  (*v*) sickness holiday credit;

  (*vi*) taxable gross pay;

  (*vii*) fixed deductions;

  (*viii*) income tax routine;

  (*ix*) employee's National Insurance contribution;

  (*x*) net pay calculation;

  (*xi*) other pay considerations;

  (*xii*) statutory holiday pay;

  (*xiii*) annual holiday pay;

  (*xiv*) advance of wages;

  (*xv*) court orders.

(*h*) Provision for input errors.

(*i*) Design of various payroll system documents.

(*j*) Payroll master file definition.

CASE STUDY III

Labour Costing

GENERAL CONSIDERATIONS

43. Introduction. Before studying the details of this case study, the reader, as before, is recommended to consider the essential elements of labour costing in a constructional engineering business, working on a number of different contracts simultaneously. This constructive approach enables the reader to consider his present thoughts and knowledge of such a system for comparison with an operational system such as the one to be outlined. As with the payroll case study it is hoped that this approach will assist the learning process which is, after all, what the study of cases is all about. Considerations should include:

(*a*) types of contracts obtained;

(*b*) definition of contract labour cost master file clearly indicating the data elements it should contain in respect of contract records;

(*c*) method of creating the initial contract master file and the procedure for dealing with amendments;

(*d*) use of check digits to provide self-checking numbers with regard to clock numbers, contract numbers, operation numbers and rate code;

(*e*) system testing procedures;

(*f*) input specification;

(*g*) other types of file required in the system including those for updating, for working file requirements and for reference purposes;

(*h*) preparation prior to processing;

(*i*) operator input;

(*j*) machine processing operations analysed into appropriate runs or routines;

(*k*) system controls, batch totals, etc.;

(*l*) output specification and layout of various documents and reports, i.e. cost reviews and completed contracts schedule.

44. Objectives. To record labour cost data on a cassette each week with regard to current contracts; to sort the labour cost data to operation number within contract number order and to update the contract labour cost cards; also to produce a weekly cost review and work in progress control report and a completed contracts schedule each month.

45. Structure of the system. The labour costing application has the following main sections:

(*a*) file creation;

(*b*) file amendments;

(*c*) recording of data on cassette weekly;

(*d*) weekly update of contract labour cost cards and weekly cost review report;

(*e*) completed contracts schedule and completed contracts control report.

The main features of these sections are outlined on the system flowcharts, (*see* Figs. 16 and 29). The processing routine is also outlined below which may be studied in conjunction with the flowchart.

46. Files used in the system. The following files are used during various stages of processing either for updating or reference purposes. The relevant files are also shown on the system flowchart (*see* Fig. 16).

(*a*) Daywork rates file (*see* Fig. 19).

(*b*) Operation description file.

(*c*) Labour cost data—weekly activity on contracts.

(*d*) Labour cost data—security copy.

(*e*) Sorted labour cost data.

(*f*) Brought forward master file—contract labour cost data (*see* Fig. 18).

(*g*) Carried forward master file—contract labour cost data.

CREATION OF CONTRACT LABOUR COST MASTER FILE

47. File creation document. From completed file creation documents the machine operator enters the appropriate data by means of the 399 keyboard. It is of course essential that all the data on the file creation document outlined in Fig. 17 is correct otherwise erroneous data will be stored on the master file.

48. File creation program. This program is used for the initial

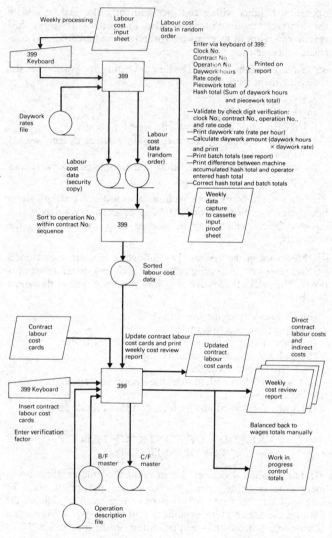

FIG. 16 *System flowchart: labour costing.*

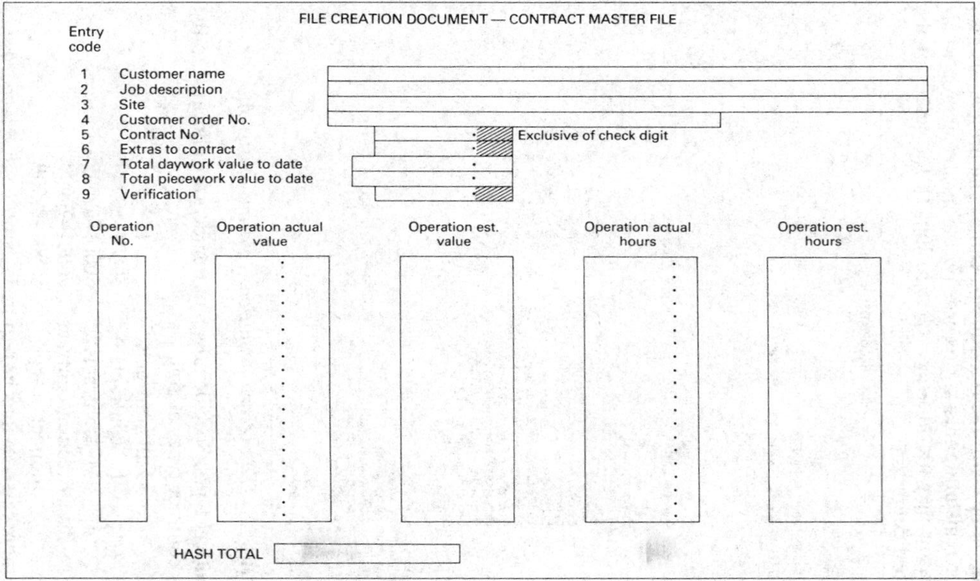

FIG. 17 *File creation document: contract master file.*

creation of contract records on the master file from data input by
the operator as indicated above. The program also prints the initial data on new contract labour cost cards. The program is also
used for reinstating missing records on the master file for whatever reason they are missing. Refer to Fig. 18 for details of the
file record definition.

FILE RECORD DEFINITION

Storage media: Cassette

Application: Labour costing

File name: Contract master file

Prepared by:

Date prepared:

Field No.	Name of field	X/N	Field length	Decimal places
1	Customer name	X	30	–
2	Job description	X	30	–
3	Site	X	30	–
4	Customer order number	X	20	–
5	Contract number	N	5	–
6	Extras to contract	N	5	–
7	Total daywork value to date	N	6	2
8	Total piecework value to date	N	6	2
9	Verification (contract No. + line No.)	N	5	–
10	Operation number × 20 (each)	N	2	–
11	Operation actual value × 20 (each)	N	6	2
12	Operation est. value × 20 (each)	N	6	–
13	Operation actual hours × 20 (each)	N	6	1
14	Operation est. hours × 20 (each)	N	6	–

Programs using this file:
   Update of contract cards
   Weekly cost review report
   Completed contracts schedule
Fields 1—6 are fixed data elements
Fields 7—14 are variable data elements

X = Alphabetic character
N = Numeric character

FIG. 18   *File record definition: contract master file.*

49. Contract types. Specific ranges of numbers are allocated to the
various contract types as follows.

Main contracts	1–9999
"F" contracts	50001–59999
"M" contracts	60001–69999
Erection contracts	70001–79999
Indirect costs	80001–89999

One or more cassettes may be required to store contract records until completed contracts are removed from the file. The maximum
number of records which can be stored on a single cassette is 250.

	I.S. FIELD NO.	NAME OF FIELD	REF	X/N	LENGTH	DP	SIGN	MAX. BYTES
1		DAYWORK RATE CODE ⎫ ×50 RATES EACH		N	2			
2		DAYWORK RATE ⎭ EACH		N	1	3		
3								
4								
5								
6								

FILE RECORD DEFINITION   CASSETTE   *

Customer   J.S. FORSTER & CO. LIMITED

Application   LABOUR COSTING

Format Name   DAYWORK RATE STATIC FILE

Prepared by: D.M. SHERREY   Date   Page   of

* Enter: Magnetic Ledger
      Cassette
      Disc
      Punched Tape
      Communications

32								
33								
34								

PROGRAMS USING THIS FILE WEEKLY CAPTURE TO CASSETTE FROM JOB TIME CARDS

TOTAL MAX. BYTES

PLUS

TOTAL RECORD BYTES

FIG. 19   *File record definition: daywork rate static file.*

FILE AMENDMENTS

50. Static data and estimated labour cost. Provision is necessary for amending fixed data on contract records as shown on the file record definition (*see* Fig. 18). Adjustments are also necessary for amending estimated labour cost to actual cost in respect of the monthly completed contracts routine (*see* **71**).

51. Transfer from one current contract to another. Provision is made for transferring incorrectly booked actual hours and value from one current contract to another. The actual hours and value taken off a contract could be transferred to more than one contract. It is also necessary to provide for balancing the data taken from one contract with the data added to correct contracts. The input of corrective entries is carried out with the following week's transactions.

CALCULATION OF CHECK DIGITS

52. Method to be used. The method selected is referred to as geometric weighting using Modulus 11 and a complement. The basic stages in calculating a check digit are outlined as follows:

(a) multiply base number (clock no., contract no., operation no., or rate code) by weighting factor;

(b) sum the products;

(c) divide result by Modulus 11 and note remainder;

(d) subtract the remainder from Modulus 11 to arrive at the check digit.

53. Example 1. Referring to the weekly data capture to cassette input proof sheet (*see* Fig. 23) clock number 105.04 is calculated in the following manner:

(a) multiply base number 105 by weighting factor:

Base No.	0	0	1	0	5 ×
Weights	10	5	8	4	2
	0	0	8	0	10

(b) sum the products:

$$0 + 0 + 8 + 0 + 10 = 18$$

(c) divide result by Modulus 11 and note remainder:

$$18 \div 11 = 1 \text{ remainder } 7$$

(d) subtract the remainder from Modulus 11 to arrive at the check digit:

$$11 - 7 = 04$$

$$\therefore \text{ Base number including check digit} = 105.04$$

54. Example 2. Also referring to the weekly data capture to cassette input proof sheet (*see* Fig. 23), clock number 97.05 is calculated as follows:

(a) multiply base number 97 by weighting factor:

Base No.	0	0	0	9	7 ×
Weights	10	5	8	4	2
	0	0	0	36	14

(b) sum the products:

$$0 + 0 + 0 + 36 + 14 = 50$$

(*c*) divide result by Modulus 11 to arrive at the remainder:

$$50 \div 11 = 4 \text{ remainder } 6$$

(*d*) subtract the remainder from Modulus 11 to arrive at the check digit:

$$11 - 6 = 05$$

∴ Base number including check digit = 97.05

TESTING PROCEDURE

55. Input data. Prior to any system going live it is necessary to ensure that it will achieve the desired results and this requires the processing of samples of input data to establish that the processed results agree with pre-compiled results.

For this particular system it was agreed that the testing routine should involve the following instructions.

(*a*) Include data for contracts for which there is no master record on the file, i.e. new contracts.

(*b*) Do not action every contract contained on the master file by omitting at least two.

(*c*) A batch of input data for testing should consist of six clock numbers and each of the employees can work on different contracts and operations at random.

(*d*) All check digits should be input in respect of the data being subjected to testing.

(*e*) Labour cost input sheet hash totals and pre-list hash totals should be calculated.

(*f*) Expected results of daywork hours × rate calculations should be compiled.

(*g*) Produce two weeks input, as it will be necessary to prove the master file updating program, over two weeks processing.

56. Run testing. Having established the elements of the system to be tested the following procedure is required.

(*a*) Using the above input data, calculate and note the expected results on the updated ledger cards, weekly cost review, work-in-progress controls and over-all contract totals. The expected results should be recorded in the same format as that to be produced by the 399 to facilitate comparisons.

(*b*) The above procedure should be repeated for the second week's input.

57. Completed contracts. At least two contracts should be completed and recorded in the same format to be produced by the 399 in respect of calculations relating to contract totals, completed contracts control and over-all totals (*see* Figs. 30–32).

WEEKLY PROCESSING ROUTINE—DATA CAPTURE TO CASSETTE—GENERAL SYSTEM REQUIREMENTS

58. Clock number. There will be only one clock number recorded on each job time card and each clock number will be validated by the process of check digit verification.

59. Job time cards and labour cost input sheet. Job time cards (*see* Figs. 20 and 21) are compiled by works employees and the accu-

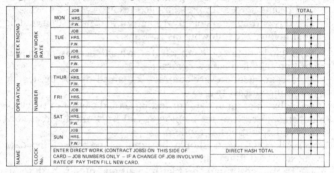

FIG. 20   *Job time card: front.*

FIG. 21   *Job time card: reverse.*

racy of hours recorded is checked by works office staff. The cards often get soiled from handling in the works which makes some of the entries illegible; this slows down the input rate by the 399 operator. What is more, inaccurate data could be input causing it to be rejected and sent back for checking and correction prior to re-entry. This of course slows down the whole data processing activity. To prevent this situation occurring the data from job time cards are transferred to labour cost input sheets compiled by office staff (*see* Fig. 22). Although this is an additional clerical

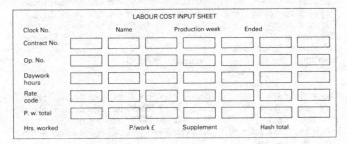

FIG. 22 *Labour cost input sheet.*
See Table VIII for specification of data fields.

operation it is deemed worthwhile as it allows processing operations to proceed more smoothly by minimising the number of rejections.

In addition, as it is possible for an employee to work on the same contract for several days or even the whole week, provision is made for summarising contract hours when transferring them from job time cards to labour cost input sheets.

The line number for each line of entry from labour cost input sheets is automatically incremented by program. Provision is made for entering a maximum of forty (average of five) contract numbers on each labour cost input sheet; accordingly forty lines of entry per labour cost input sheet are catered for before encoding to cassette. Each employee will normally work on one operation type per labour cost input sheet but could occasionally work on more than one.

60. Daywork rate code. Daywork rates are generally related to operation type, with minor exceptions. The first rate entered from each labour cost input sheet is retained until another rate

TABLE VIII. SPECIFICATION OF DATA FIELDS—WEEKLY DATA CAPTURE
TO CASSETTE INPUT PROOF SHEET

Field	Type of character	Number of characters
Clock number	Numeric	999.99 inc. two check digits
Line number	Numeric	99
Contract number	Numeric	99999.99 inc. two check digits
Operation number	Numeric	99.99 inc. two check digits
Daywork hours	Numeric	999.9 inc. one decimal place
Daywork rate code	Numeric	99.99 inc. two check digits
Daywork amount	Numeric	999.99 inc. two decimal places
Piecework total	Numeric	999.99 inc. two decimal places
Labour cost input sheet hash total	Numeric	9999.99
Batch totals:		
Daywork hours	Numeric	99999.9 inc. one decimal place
Daywork amount	Numeric	99999.99 inc. two decimal places
Piecework amount	Numeric	99999.99 inc. two decimal places
Batch hash total (sum of daywork hours and piecework amount)	Numeric	999999.99 inc. two decimal places
Pre-list hash total	Numeric	999999.99 inc. two decimal places
Difference	Numeric	As appropriate (*see* Fig. 23)

code is entered. The rate is cleared upon completion of each
labour cost input sheet.

PROCESSING ACTIVITIES

61. Preparation for processing. The machine operator attends to
the following requirements.

(*a*) Select and load program.

(*b*) Select and load three cassette stations with the daywork
rates file, and two labour cost data cassettes including security
copy. Rates are loaded into the machine's memory at the beginning of the routine (*see* Figs. 16 and 19).

(*c*) Load weekly data capture to cassette input proof sheet
stationery (*see* Fig. 23).

(*d*) Select batch of labour cost input sheets (*see* Fig. 22).

WEEKLY DATA CAPTURE TO CASSETTE INPUT PROOF SHEET

CLOCK NO.	LINE NO.	CONTRACT NO.	OPERATION NO.	DAYWORK HOURS	DAYWORK RATE CODE	DAYWORK RATE	DAYWORK AMOUNT	PIECEWORK TOTAL	LABOUR COST INPUT SHEET HASH TOTAL
105.04	1	1453.03	7.08	6.5	14.10	1.500	9.75	2.00	
(See 11)	2	1094.06	7.08	10.0	14.10	1.500	15.00		
	3	52067.01	15.08	12.0	2.07	1.755	21.06		
	4	65431.01	7.08	11.0	14.10	1.500	16.50	4.25	45.75
				*39.5				*6.25	
97.05	1	2347.02	13.01	25.2	9.04	1.256	31.65		
(See 12)	2	70154.04	16.06	10.0	12.03	1.350	13.50		
ERROR LINE	2	70154.04	16.06	10.0	12.03	1.350	13.50		
CORR. LINE	3	70154.04	16.06	15.0	12.03	1.350	20.25		60.20
				*60.2					
175.09	1	1756.06	17.04	16.0	5.01	1.629	26.06	5.00	
	2	53125.08	17.04	5.5	5.01	1.629	8.96		36.50
ERR.HASH TOTAL				*21.5				*11.25	36.50CR
CORR.HASH TOTAL				*121.2					26.50

BATCH TOTALS	
DAYWORK HOURS	121.2
DAYWORK AMOUNT	149.23
PIECEWORK AMOUNT	11.25
BATCH HASH TOTAL	132.45**
PRE-LIST HASH TOTAL	132.45
DIFFERENCE	.00

FIG. 23 *Weekly data capture to cassette input proof sheet.*
* These figures are not printed but are shown to enable the reader to appreciate the manner of obtaining batch totals.
** 121.2 + 11.25 = 132.45.

62. Operator input. From the batch of labour cost input sheets (*see* Fig. 22), the operator enters the following data by means of the N.C.R. 399 keyboard:

    (*a*) clock number;
    (*b*) contract number;
    (*c*) operation number;
    (*d*) daywork hours;
    (*e*) day rate code;
    (*f*) piecework total;
    (*g*) hash total.

All of these data elements are printed on the weekly data capture to cassette input proof sheet (*see* Figs. 16 and 23). The operator then enters the labour cost input sheet hash total which is the sum of daywork hours and piecework total. When the batch of sheets is completed the operator enters the pre-list batch hash total into the machine (*see* **63** (*d*)).

63. Machine operations. Having set up the job and entered labour cost data the machine then performs the following operations automatically (*see* Fig. 16).

(*a*) Validate by means of check digit verification the clock number, contract number, operation number and rate code. Incorrect entries are not printed.

(*b*) Select and print daywork rate by reference to daywork rate code.

(*c*) Calculate daywork amount by multiplying daywork hours by the daywork rate. The amount is printed on the weekly data capture to cassette input proof sheet. Daywork hours are converted to decimals of whole hours and the daywork amount is rounded to the nearest whole penny. Parts of an hour are expressed in units of six minutes; therefore 1.1 is equal to one hour and six minutes and 1.2 is equal to one hour and twelve minutes, etc.

(*d*) The machine derives and compares the labour cost input sheet hash total with the predetermined hash total entered by the operator. The difference is printed on the weekly data capture to cassette input proof sheet summary (*see* Fig. 23). On non-agreement provision is made either to reverse automatically incorrect line(s) by indexing incorrect line number or to reject automatically the entire record. Provision is also made to correct the hash total when necessary (*see* Fig. 23).

(*e*) When each batch of labour cost input sheets has been completed the following totals are printed on the weekly data capture to cassette input proof sheet (*see* Fig. 23):

(*i*) daywork hours;

(*ii*) daywork amount;

(*iii*) piecework amount;

(*iv*) batch hash total (sum of daywork hours column and piecework total column);

(*v*) pre-list hash total.

(*f*) The machine accumulated batch hash total is compared with the pre-list hash total entered by the operator. Any difference between the two figures is printed on the weekly data capture to cassette input proof sheet (*see* Fig. 23).

(*g*) The validated data is recorded on a labour cost data cassette in random order and a security copy is produced simultaneously.

(*h*) The data in random order on the labour cost data cassette is then sorted by a sort program into operation number within contract number sequence. The sorted data is recorded on a cassette.

64. Weekly data capture to cassette input proof sheet. Details of data fields are shown in Table VIII which should be studied in conjunction with Fig. 23.

WEEKLY PROCESSING ROUTINE—WEEKLY UPDATING OF CONTRACT LABOUR COST CARDS AND WEEKLY COST REVIEW REPORT

65. Preparation for processing. The machine operator attends to the following requirements (*see* Fig. 16).

(*a*) Select and load program.

(*b*) Select and load brought forward master file—contract labour cost data, the cassette for recording updated records (the carried forward file) and the operation description file.

(*c*) Select and load contract labour cost cards. These cards are non-magnetic and there is a separate card for each contract.

(*d*) Load weekly cost review stationery.

(*e*) Load sorted labour cost data cassette.

66. Operator input. From the contract labour cost cards (*see* Fig.

24) the operator enters the verification factor for comparison with the verification factor on the contract labour cost data master file. This is to ensure the selection of the correct contract labour cost card for updating purposes.

LABOUR COST CARD									
CONTRACT No.									
WEEK ENDING DATE	CLOCK No.	DAY-WORK HOURS	DAY-WORK		PIECEWORK VALUE	OPERATION TOTALS TO DATE			VERIFICATION
			RATE	VALUE		HOURS	VALUE	OPER.	
		SPECIFICATION	OF	DATA	FIELDS				
DDMMMYY	999	999·9	9·999	999·99	9999·99	999999·9	9999999·99		
T ALPHA NUMERIC 3N	3N	3N+1D.P.	1N+3D.P.	3N+2D.P.	4N+2D.P.	6N+1D.P.	6N+2D.P.	4 ALPHA	

FIG. 24 *Labour cost card.*

67. Machine operations. Having set up the job and verified that the the correct contract labour cost card has been inserted in the machine, the machine automatically updates the brought forward master file cassette and produces the carried forward cassette. The summarised labour cost data for the week is printed on the contract labour cost card. The printed details include daywork hours, daywork value and piecework value for each man, within an operation type for a contract (*see* Fig. 24).

As a man's daywork rate does not change unless he works on another operation, the summarised hours and value for each man will also be by daywork rate. Upon completion of updating a contract labour cost card, only those "operation totals to date" (*see* Fig. 24) affected during the week will be printed on the card.

On opening a new card all brought forward operation totals to date are printed. Should a contract number not exist on the master file during the master file updating run, provision is made for creating a contract labour cost card, inserting the contract number on the master file in the correct numerical position and posting the current week's data to the card, master file and weekly cost review. An indication is shown on the weekly cost review that the contract number did not exist on the master file so that the situation can subsequently be investigated. The file creation and amendment programs will cater for adding new contract numbers to the master file and contract labour cost cards.

WEEKLY COST REVIEW – DIRECT OPERATIONS

CONTRACT NO 2777
CUSTOMER NAME (Omitted for confidentiality)
JOB DESCRIPTION REPAIRS TO ROD/BAR MILL RECUP
SITE SHOP
EXTRAS TO CONTRACT
CUSTOMER ORDER NO

OPERATION DESCRIPTION	ACTUAL VALUE	ESTIMATED VALUE	ACTUAL HOURS	ESTIMATED HOURS	TOTAL DAYWORK VALUE TO DATE	TOTAL PIECEWORK VALUE TO DATE
PLTM	1479.18		800.6			
SHER	139.95		80.3			
BURN	40.25		23.5			
SAW	142.74		104.5			
CROP	122.67		99.0			
HOLE	273.12		224.9			
MACH	685.79		461.0			
PLAN	4.56		2.5			
WELD	1908.20		972.1			
MIGW	166.29		73.4			
CCRT	154.89		72.0			
FIN	15.99		11.9			
FORM	233.07		124.8			
SDS	678.35		441.0			
CONTRACT TOTALS	6045.05		3491.5		4621.38	1423.67

FIG. 25 *Weekly cost review: direct operations.*

WEEKLY COST REVIEW – INDIRECT OPERATIONS

CONTRACT NO   82677
CUSTOMER NAME
JOB DESCRIPTION
SITE
EXTRAS TO CONTRACT
CUSTOMER ORDER NO

OPERATION DESCRIPTION	ACTUAL VALUE	ESTIMATED VALUE	ACTUAL HOURS	ESTIMATED HOURS	TOTAL DAYWORK VALUE TO DATE	TOTAL PIECEWORK VALUE TO DATE
GL	357.79		299.8			
OC	480.12		443.4			
PM	263.90		192.9			
WT	255.43		207.5			
TL	146.36		112.0			
SM	144.68		130.7			
SW	115.99		117.4			
WS	59.42		86.2			
CL	48.00		72.4			
BM	60.42		30.0			
SH	2.38		2.0			
TR	17.18		36.4			
SCH	7.95		8.0			
OJ	7.79		6.0			
SS	9.26		6.0			
SY	12.88		12.5			
(See Fig. 21)						
CONTRACT TOTALS	1989.55		1763.2		1623.29	366.26

FIG. 26   *Weekly cost review: indirect operations.*

Three copies of the weekly cost review report are printed automatically on continuous perforated paper fed by a continuous forms feeder. Reviews are printed for both direct and indirect operations (*see* Figs. 27 and 28).

The balances for each operation for each contract represent the previous balances plus the current week's activity including those operation totals to date that have not been affected by the current week's activity. Work in progress control totals are required at the end of each contract type (*see* Fig. 16). Up to twenty operation descriptions of four alpha characters each, for each contract type is provided for. The operation descriptions for any contract type may be different (*see* Figs. 27 and 28).

68. Weekly cost review, work in progress control and over-all control totals. Details of data fields are shown in Table IX which should be studied in conjunction with Figs. 25–28.

69. Indirect costs. Indirect costs for purposes of programming are regarded as a contract type and are allocated to indirect cost code analysed over twenty heads. By incrementing the last indirect cost code by one each week (for data capture and master file), the weekly cost review shows the indirect costs for each week of the year. This procedure allows indirect costs to be dealt with in the same manner as ordinary contracts (*see* Figs. 21 and 26).

70. Extras to contracts. Within each contract type range a series of consecutive contract numbers is set aside to which are posted additional costs to original contracts. The contract numbers allocated for additional costs are encoded in the "Extras to Contracts" section of the fixed data of the original contract on the master file and labour cost card. This is achieved by means of the file amendment program (*see* Figs. 18 and 24).

The original contract number is encoded in the "Extras to Contracts" section of the fixed data of the contract or contracts containing the additional costs. This is achieved during the file creation of the additional costs contracts.

All the "Extras to Contracts" cost information relating to the original contract is printed on the weekly cost review in the correct contract type range and in sequence, although there will be a gap on the report between the original contract and its associated additional costs.

WORK IN PROGRESS CONTROL – DIRECT OPERATIONS

OPERATION DESCRIPTION	ACTUAL VALUE	ACTUAL HOURS	TOTAL DAYWORK VALUE TO DATE	TOTAL PIECEWORK VALUE TO DATE
NCFC	.00	.0		
PLTM	17077.05	8664.4		
SHER	1172.82	735.3		
BURN	3029.97	1568.6		
SAW	427.79	300.9		
CROP	435.09	333.0		
HOLE	1713.80	1197.5		
MACH	821.00	536.7		
PLAN	1262.20	580.7		
WELD	10531.38	5421.2		
MIGW	1378.20	752.0		
CCRT	1115.81	538.0		
FIN	879.36	532.8		
TRPT	.00	.0		
FORM	3215.19	1600.1		
EST	.00	.0		
EXP	.00	.0		
EREC	.00	.0		
MCDR	5.44	4.0		
SDS	854.01	525.5		
OVER-ALL CONTRACT TOTALS	43919.11	23290.7	33606.24	10312.87

FIG. 27   Work in progress control: direct operations.

TABLE IX. SPECIFICATION OF DATA FIELDS—WEEKLY COST REVIEW,
WORK IN PROGRESS CONTROL AND OVER-ALL CONTROL TOTALS

Field	Type of character	Number of characters
Weekly cost review (*see* Figs. 25 and 26):		
Contract number	Numeric	99999 (check digits not printed)
Customer name	Alpha	30
Job description	Alpha	30
Site	Alpha	30
Extras to contract	Numeric	99999
Customer order number	Alphanumeric	20
Operation description		4 (direct operations, *see* Fig. 25)
		2 (indirect operations, *see* Fig. 26)
Operation actual value	Numeric	999999.99 inc. two decimal places
Operation estimated value	Numeric	999999
Operation actual hours	Numeric	999999.9 inc. one decimal place
Operation estimated hours	Numeric	999999
Total daywork value to date	Numeric	999999.99 inc. two decimal places
Total piecework value to date (*see* Fig. 18)	Numeric	999999.99 inc. two decimal places
Work in progress control (*see* Figs. 27 and 28):		
Operation total to date:		
Actual value	Numeric	9999999.99 inc. two decimal places
Actual hours	Numeric	9999999.9 inc. one decimal place
Total daywork value to date	Numeric	9999999.99 inc. two decimal places
Total piecework value to date	Numeric	9999999.99 inc. two decimal places
Over-all contract totals (*see* Figs. 27 and 28):		
Actual value	Numeric	9999999.99 inc. two decimal places
Actual hours	Numeric	9999999.9 inc. one decimal place
Total daywork value to date	Numeric	9999999.99 inc. two decimal places
Total piecework value to date	Numeric	9999999.99 inc. two decimal places

WORK IN PROGRESS CONTROL – INDIRECT OPERATIONS

OPERATION DESCRIPTION	ACTUAL VALUE	ACTUAL HOURS	TOTAL DAYWORK VALUE TO DATE	TOTAL PIECEWORK VALUE TO DATE
GL	2569.17	1753.1		
OC	3775.59	2850.9		
PM	2685.97	1512.2		
WT	4610.13	2828.2		
TL	885.06	590.6		
SM	777.60	530.2		
SW	796.88	579.4		
WS	342.60	405.9		
CL	331.59	413.5		
BM	195.53	122.0		
SH	32.32	23.4		
TR	181.41	197.3		
SCH	120.95	80.0		
OJ	.00	.0		
SS	.00	.0		
PI	22.65	14.5		
ST	10.85	.0		
SDS	103.04	48.0		
SY	211.08	134.3		
	.00	.0		
OVER-ALL CONTRACT TOTALS	17652.42	12083.5	15590.17	2062.25

FIG. 28 Work in progress control: indirect operations.

COMPLETED CONTRACTS ROUTINE

71. Weekly clerical routine. Each week the sales book is checked for completed contracts for the purpose of recording the actual labour cost and the estimated value. The relevant contract labour cost card is extracted from the file and transferred to a completed contracts file (*see* Fig. 29).

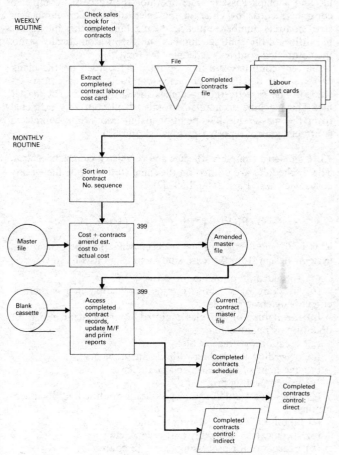

FIG. 29 *System flowchart: completed contracts routine.*

72. Monthly routine. At the end of the month contract labour cost cards in the completed file are manually sorted into contract number sequence. In respect of cost-plus contracts it is necessary to amend the most recent master file containing contract labour cost data by adjusting the estimated labour cost to actual cost. The machine operator then loads the machine with the amended file and a blank cassette. The operator then accesses completed contract records by entering the relevant contract number in strict contract number sequence, the machine searches the master file to locate the contract number and then automatically prints the completed contracts schedule (*see* Fig. 29).

Current contracts still in progress are recorded on the blank cassette, but details of completed contracts are of course excluded. The cassette then becomes the current contract master file. The machine accumulates totals of all contracts extracted from the master file by operation detail and prints completed contracts control reports (*see* Figs. 31 and 32).

73. Completed contracts schedule and completed contracts control. These schedules are printed on the same stationery as the weekly cost review (*see* Figs. 25 and 30–32).

OVERVIEW OF CASE STUDY III

This is to enable the reader to check what has been learnt of systems design from this case study and as a basis for review:

(*a*) specification of system objectives;

(*b*) structure of a labour costing application in a structural engineering environment;

(*c*) the nature of the files required in the system either for updating or reference purposes;

(*d*) creation of a master file;

(*e*) procedure for dealing with file amendments;

(*f*) methods of calculating check digits;

(*g*) system testing procedure;

(*h*) labour cost data capture processing routine and documentation;

(*i*) labour cost card updating routine;

(*j*) specification of weekly cost review, etc.;

(*k*) procedure for processing extras to contract;

(*l*) completed contracts routine.

COMPLETED CONTRACTS SCHEDULE

CONTRACT NO	3015
CUSTOMER NAME	(omitted for confidentiality)
JOB DESCRIPTION	4-COMPLETE SETS INTNALS
SITE	SHOP
ESTRAS TO CONTRACT	
CUSTOMER ORDER NO	HB7147/C62/R1255

OP. DESC	ACTUAL VALUE	EST. VALUE	VARIANCE AMOUNT	PERCENTAGE OF ACTUAL TO EST.	ACTUAL HOURS	EST. HOURS	TOT D/WORK VALUE	TOT P/WORK VALUE
PLTM	1171.38		1171.38	.00	611.4			
SHER	125.94		125.94	.00	89.1			
BURN	6.59		6.59	.00	4.0			
CROP	47.16		47.16	.00	35.1			
HOLE	2.01		2.01	.00	1.5			
PLAN	278.04		278.04	.00	128.6			
WELD	1973.92		1973.92	.00	1027.4			
FIN	9.25		9.25	.00	6.0			
FORM	462.12		462.12	.00	225.2			
EST	.00	3272	3272	.00	.0			
CONT TOTS	4076.41	3272	801E	124.57	2128.3		3132.39	944.02

FIG. 30 Completed contracts schedule.

COMPLETED CONTRACTS CONTROL — DIRECT OPERATIONS

OP. DESC	ACTUAL VALUE	EST. VALUE	VARIANCE AMOUNT	PERCENTAGE OF ACTUAL TO EST.	ACTUAL HOURS	EST. HOURS	TOT D/WORK VALUE	TOT P/WORK VALUE
NCFC	.00			.00	.0			
PLTM	1620.22		1620%	.00	822.1			
SHER	74.95		74%	.00	49.3			
BURN	250.04	94	156%	265.95	119.7			
SAW	4.04		4%	.00	3.0			
CROP	2.68		2%	.00	2.0			
HOLE	211.48		211%	.00	146.0			
MACH	105.51		105%	.00	57.7			
PLAN	112.51	70	42%	160.00	51.8			
WELD	1487.98		1487%	.00	731.2			
MIGW	274.65		274%	.00	166.7			
CCRT	122.95		122%	.00	64.0			
FIN	28.63		28%	.00	13.8			
TRPT	.00			.00	.0			
FORM	453.00	48	405%	943.75	230.7			
EST	.00	4012	4012	.00	.0			
EXP	.00			.00	.0			
EREC	.00			.00	.0			
MCDR	.00			.00	.0			
SDS	.00			.00	.0			
OVER-ALL TOTALS	4748.64	4224	518%	112.40	2458.0		3639.54	1109.10

FIG. 31 Completed contracts control: direct operations.

COMPLETED CONTRACTS CONTROL – INDIRECT OPERATIONS

OP. DESC	ACTUAL VALUE	EST. VALUE	VARIANCE AMOUNT	PERCENTAGE OF ACTUAL TO EST.	ACTUAL HOURS	EST. HOURS	TOT D/WORK VALUE	TOT P/WORK VALUE
GL	1710.16		1710 CR	.00	1167.7			
OC	2614.42		2614 CR	.00	1976.7			
PM	1839.80		1839 CR	.00	1044.3			
WT	3560.51		3560 CR	.00	2184.2			
TL	576.43		576 CR	.00	385.9			
SM	543.42		543 CR	.00	370.5			
SW	524.12		524 CR	.00	393.1			
WS	232.80		232 CR	.00	271.4			
CL	211.95		211 CR	.00	264.3			
BM	7.46		7 CR	.00	4.0			
SH	17.18		17 CR	.00	9.0			
TR	75.45		75 CR	.00	67.9			
SCH	84.43		84 CR	.00	56.0			
OJ	.00			.00	.0			
SS	.00			.00	10.0			
PI	15.15		15 CR	.00	.0			
ST	5.12		5 CR	.00	24.0			
SDS	63.65		63 CR	.00	87.3			
SY	137.21		137 CR	.00	.0			
OVER-ALL TOTALS	12219.26		12212 CR	.00	8316.3		10775.79	1443.47

FIG. 32   Completed contracts control: indirect operations.

Steel Making: On-Line Order Processing and Related Sub-Systems

GENERAL CONSIDERATIONS

1. Company profile. The company to which this case study relates wishes to remain anonymous for reasons of policy but it is sufficient to say that the company is concerned with the manufacture of steel plate and sections. The various processes include electric arc furnaces equipped for automatic power input control and an interface for future computer control.

The policy of the company is to develop not only to meet changes in market conditions and to take advantage of technological change, but to provide sufficient growth to maintain adequate profitability and return on capital employed.

The case study to be outlined embraces only a part of the computerised systems which support the steelmaking operations.

2. Outline of application. This case study is predominantly concerned with on-line order processing, or an on-line order book, as it may be called. The system details, however, are expanded to indicate the relationship of other sub-systems which utilise order details in a batch processing mode. The sub-systems include the following.

(*a*) On-line entry of order details, calculation of order weights, validation of account details and order dimensions, pricing of steel and calculation of carriage.

(*b*) On-line entry of order details and data in respect of cast analysis and planning requirements. Output of works documentation direct to the planning office and section mill office for stock orders.

(*c*) Batch processing of orders and production of customer documentation and works documentation in respect of the current rolling week. Production of list of accounts which have exceeded the allowed credit limit.

(*d*) Batch processing of invoices, updating sales ledger and production of statements.

(*e*) Batch processing of miscellaneous sales items.

(*f*) Customer master file amendments.

(*g*) Order intake analysis.

3. Reasons for converting to an on-line order processing system.
The main reasons for replacing the original computerised batch processing system and related clerical operations with an on-line system are summarised below.

(*a*) Order acknowledgments and amendments and works documents can be produced automatically thereby saving typists' time in the sales office.

(*b*) On-line videos and termiprinters ensure that orders for delivery from stock are received by the mills for processing much faster than by other means.

(*c*) Various reports can now be produced which were not easy to obtain previously.

(*d*) The need to have comptometer operators in the sales office to calculate order weights is eliminated.

(*e*) The original system which allowed the company to input orders to a computer by means of punched cards, required between twelve and twenty-six cards to be punched and verified. This situation is now eliminated.

(*f*) The number of cards required to update the sales ledger system was reduced by 75 per cent.

(*g*) Invoices are produced automatically thus saving typists' time in the accounts department, although there still exists a need for processing a small percentage of invoices manually.

(*h*) Statistical information is produced more accurately.

(*i*) A computerised order processing system allowed a Blooming Mill planning system to be introduced. The details of this system are contained in the author's companion HAND-BOOK *Business Systems* (*see* Appendix III).

4. Computer configuration.
The computer configuration on which the application is processed consists of an I.C.L. 1902A with an internal memory capacity of 48K. The peripherals include:

(*a*) one 300 c.p.m. card reader which is only used for the input of parameter cards to the batch processing element of the order processing system;

(b) one 600 l.p.m. printer used for printing various lists and documents;

(c) four tape drives which are not used in the order processing system;

(d) three E.D.S. 30 (disc drives) used for on-line processing requirements;

(e) four V.D.U.s. Two of the videos are in the sales department and are used to calculate order weights, check account details and update the on-line order book. One video is located in the planning office and is used to put the planning details onto orders and input cast details and planning details. The fourth video is used as a spare;

(f) two termiprinters. One termiprinter is used to output the works documentation direct to the planning office and section mill office to speed the dispatch of stock orders (see Fig. 33).

OUTLINE OF ORDER PROCESSING ROUTINE

The following details should be read in conjunction with Fig. 33.

5. Sales department. An order is received by the sales department either verbally or by letter. The sales desk then write the details on an order pro-forma (see Fig. 34).

6. Screen 2. As a customer usually orders either a number of plates of a certain dimension or orders a specific tonnage, it is necessary to calculate the exact weight of the plate and of the order. The order is therefore passed to a video operator who calls up screen 2 on the video and enters the dimensions of the order and the account number of the customer. An order can be entered in imperial format and it will be converted to the metric equivalent; the weight will then be calculated. There are fields on the screen for "less percentage" and "extra percentage" on length and width, and these are taken into account if necessary. If an order is of undesirable dimensions to produce, a message is flashed on the screen to this effect so that the sales desk can be informed and decide whether to accept or reject the order.

If any of the fields contain invalid data an appropriate error message is output on the screen. The account number entered is checked against the customer master file (custom real: file 1) to

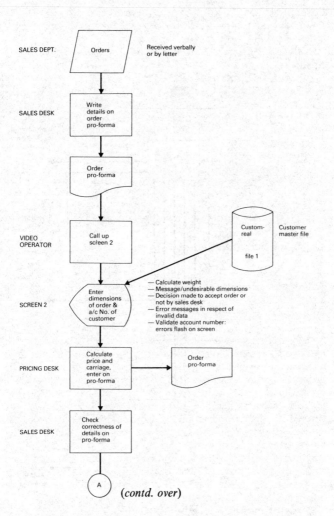

FIG. 33 *Outline flowchart of on-line order processing routine.*

SALES DEPT. — Orders — Received verbally or by letter

SALES DESK — Write details on order pro-forma

Order pro-forma

VIDEO OPERATOR — Call up screen 2

Customer master file — Customer-real file 1

SCREEN 2 — Enter dimensions of order & a/c No. of customer
— Calculate weight
— Message/undesirable dimensions
— Decision made to accept order or not by sales desk
— Error messages in respect of invalid data
— Validate account number: errors flash on screen

PRICING DESK — Calculate price and carriage, enter on pro-forma

Order pro-forma

SALES DESK — Check correctness of details on pro-forma

A

(contd. over)

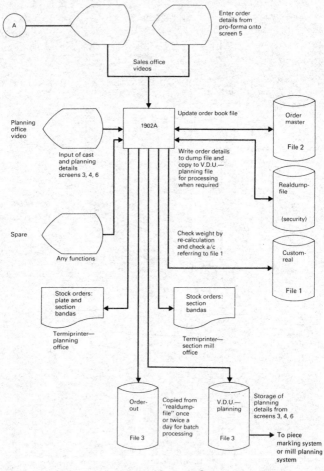

FIG. 33—contd.

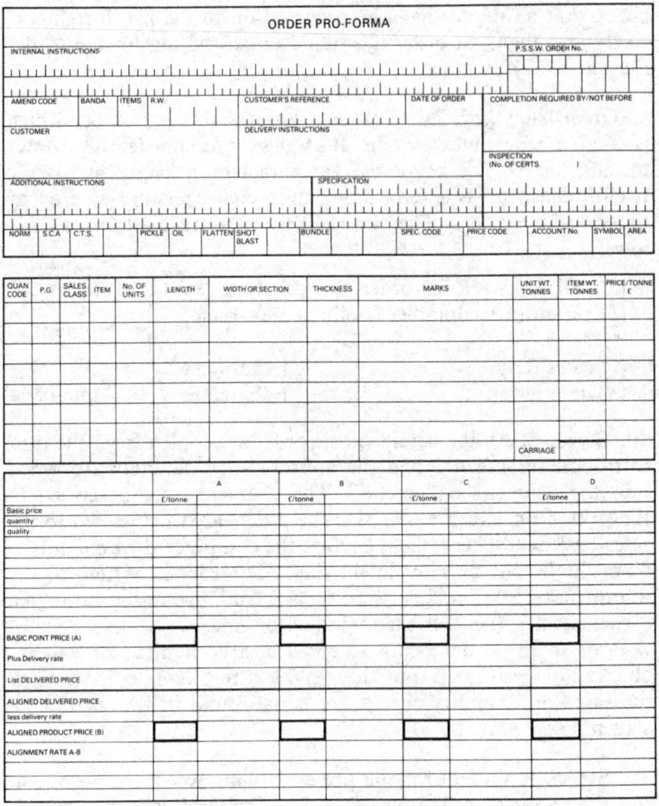
ORDER PRO-FORMA
INTERNAL INSTRUCTIONS
P.S.S.W. ORDER No.
AMEND CODE
BANDA
ITEMS
R.W.
CUSTOMER'S REFERENCE
DATE OF ORDER
COMPLETION REQUIRED BY/NOT BEFORE
CUSTOMER
DELIVERY INSTRUCTIONS
INSPECTION (No. OF CERTS.)
ADDITIONAL INSTRUCTIONS
SPECIFICATION
NORM
S.C.A
C.T.S.
PICKLE
OIL
FLATTEN
SHOT BLAST
BUNDLE
SPEC. CODE
PRICE CODE
ACCOUNT No.
SYMBOL
AREA
QUAN CODE
P.G.
SALES CLASS
ITEM
No. OF UNITS
LENGTH
WIDTH OR SECTION
THICKNESS
MARKS
UNIT WT. TONNES
ITEM WT. TONNES
PRICE/TONNE £
CARRIAGE
A
B
C
D
£/tonne
£/tonne
£/tonne
£/tonne
Basic price
quantity
quality
BASIC POINT PRICE (A)
Plus Delivery rate
List DELIVERED PRICE
ALIGNED DELIVERED PRICE
less delivery rate
ALIGNED PRODUCT PRICE (B)
ALIGNMENT RATE A-B

FIG. 34 *Order pro-forma.*

see if the account is valid. Any errors are indicated on the screen of the video and are set to flash so that the operator's attention is attracted immediately.

7. Pricing desk. Once the weight is calculated and the account checked the order is passed across to the pricing desk where the price of the steel and the carriage rate are calculated and entered on the pro-forma (*see* Fig. 33).

8. Sales desk. The order then goes back to the sales desk who

check that all details have been copied on to the pro-forma correctly and then the order is entered on to the master file (order
master: file 2) by video.

9. Order index key. Every order is given a unique number which
is used as the index key on the sales order master file (order
master: file 2). The key is twelve characters in length but as the
twelfth character is a zero, only eleven characters are entered by
the video operators. The eleven characters are made up as follows:

(a) delivery week for order	– 4 characters	
(b) actual order number (Folio No.)	– 5 characters	Numeric
(c) sales desk	– 1 character	
(d) item letter	– 1 character	Alphabetic

10. Screen 5. All the details of the order are copied from the pro-
forma on to screen 5 and the appropriate characters are typed
into the field called "amend". The characters are described in
the section on screen 5 (*see* **31**). The orders are then passed to the
sales desk who check them against the computer documentation
from the batch run later in the day. The order is written to the
dump file (realdumpfile: security file) and the order book file
(order master: file 2) is then updated on-line.

Prior to the order being accepted a large number of validity
checks are performed and the weight is re-calculated. All error
messages and validity checks are to be found in the section on
screen 5 (*see* **31**).

11. Screen 6. Orders for the present rolling week are output to
this screen for planning purposes. For further details of screen 6,
see **32**.

12. Termiprinters. Stock orders are output to termiprinters in the
planning office and section mill office. All the records for output
to the termiprinters are held on the dump file. The sub-routine
C∅35—TERMSELECT reads the dump file to see if there are
any orders to be output. It will signal the previous record output
as being processed so that it will not be output again unless spe-
cifically asked for. Sub-routines C∅36—TERMSETUP will move
the data from the input/output area to the message area for
output to the terminal (*see* Figs. 33, 35 and 36).

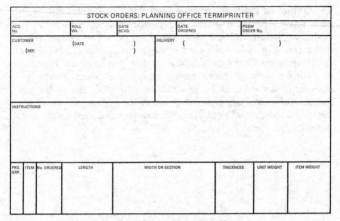

FIG. 35   *Stock orders: planning office termiprinter.*

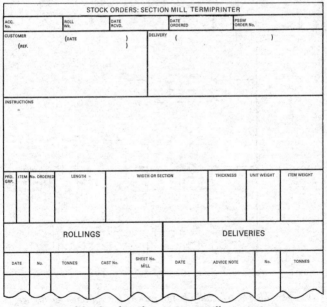

FIG. 36   *Stock orders: section mill termiprinter.*

13. Outline of daily batch processing routine. A batch job is run each day to produce works and customer documentation. The customer documentation takes the form of acknowledgments of order (*see* Fig. 38) and order amendments (*see* Fig. 39) for all orders processed. These documents are produced in triplicate: one copy is sent to the customer, the second is sent to the area sales representative and the third is filed with the order pro-forma in the sales department. A list of the orders processed with details of the amendment type is produced and filed in the computer department (*see* Fig. 37).

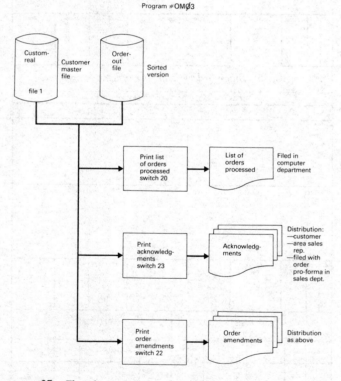

FIG. 37   *Flowchart: daily batch processing routine—customer documentation.*

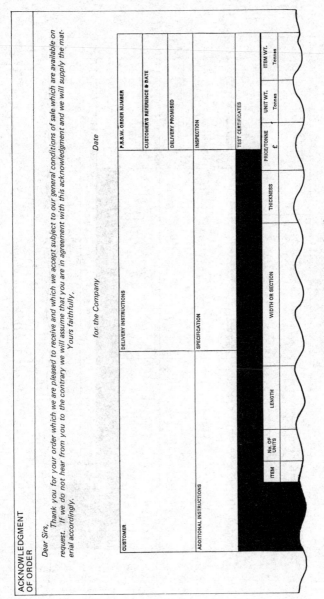

FIG. 38   *Acknowledgment of order.*

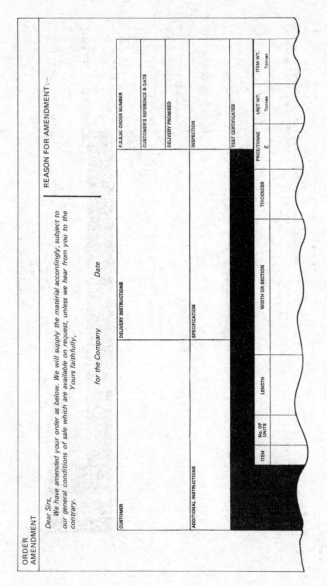

FIG. 39 Order amendment.

It has been stated above that stock orders in the form of bandas are produced on termiprinters whereas bandas for orders to be produced in the present planning week are produced during the batch run. (The term "banda" is a carry-over from the previous system when order details were produced on spirit masters and copies were duplicated from the master.)

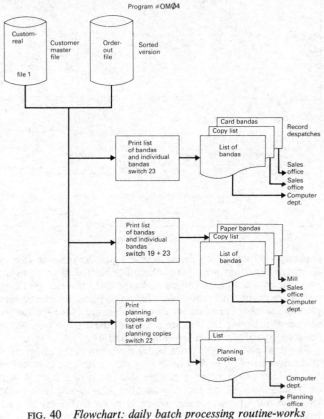

FIG. 40 *Flowchart: daily batch processing routine-works documentation.*

Two sets of bandas are produced on one card to be used as record cards in the sales department and the other on paper for

use in the mill. Both sets of bandas together with a list of bandas
are sent to the sales office for distribution (*see* Figs. 41 and 42).

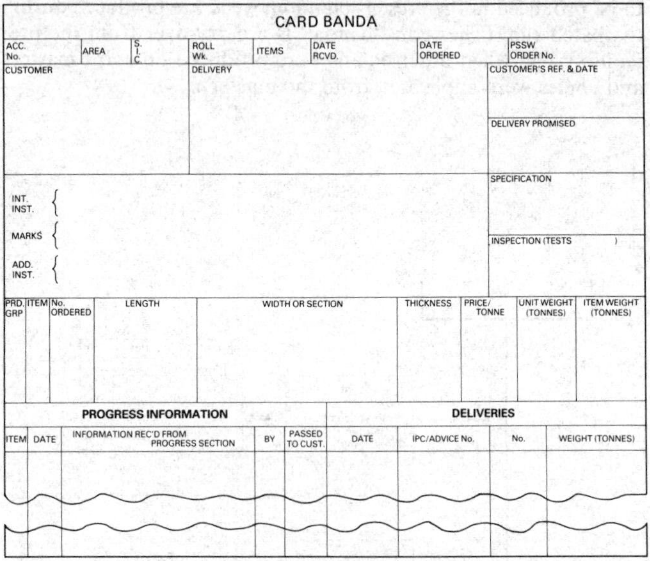

FIG. 41   *Card banda.*

One copy is retained by the sales office and the other is filed in
the computer department. The sales office has the facility to sup-
press the production of bandas and type them instead. Planning
copies are produced for all orders for prime plates for the present
planning weeks. These are sent to the planning office for the insertion of planning information. A list of these is kept on file in
the computer department (*see* Figs. 40 and 43).

The final phase of the batch order entry run is the production
of credit control data. Any orders for rolling now or to be taken
ex-stock have their value calculated and added to a control field
on the customer master file. Any accounts that exceed their credit
limit are output on a report which is given to the credit controller. This report is used to keep a reasonably accurate check of
the customers' balances.

14. Weekly runs. Bandas and planning copies are also produced
on weekly runs. When a weekly run has been done it is necessary

ACC. No.	AREA	S. I. C.	ROLL Wk.	ITEMS	DATE RCVD.	DATE ORDERED	PSSW ORDER No.

CUSTOMER

DELIVERY

CUSTOMER'S REF. & DATE

DELIVERY PROMISED

SPECIFICATION

INSTRUCTIONS

INT. INST.

MARKS

ADD INST.

INSPECTION (TESTS —)

PRD. GRP.	ITEM	No. ORDERED	LENGTH	WIDTH OR SECTION	THICKNESS	PRICE/TONNE	UNIT WEIGHT (TONNES)	ITEM WEIGHT (TONNES)

FIG. 42 *Paper banda.*

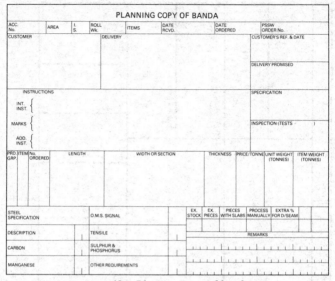

FIG. 43 *Planning copy of banda.*

to change the planning week in the on-line system to ensure that planning copies for the present week are produced. The weekly credit control run is also done at this time to readjust the control figures on the customer master file to give greater accuracy.

The orders then pass through the mill planning system to produce details of steel to be used for the order. This is followed by the invoicing and accounting routines which are discussed later (*see* **37–46**).

BATCH PROCESSING RUNS—FURTHER DETAILS

15. Order-out file. Prior to an order being written to the order book file (order-master) it is also written to a security file. *See* order master: file 2 and realdumpfile: security, Fig. 33. Once or twice a day these orders are copied from the dump file to a copy of Order-out so that batch processing can be performed from it. The dump file is then cleared of any records no longer needed for processing (*see* Fig. 33). In the batch run the file, Order-out, is filled with end records (*see* **22**) by a program referred to as

#PFIL. This is done in case the copy from the dump file fails to close the Order-out file correctly and thus ensures that spurious data (i.e. data from previous runs) is not left on the file. The "end" records will overwrite all previous data and be ignored by the program processing the file.

An end record is also written to one of the work files by the program #PFIL. This is done because the copy from the dump file will place an end of file tag after the last record it has copied out to Order-out and there must always be an end record on a file for it to be acceptable to the data processing standards.

The purpose of the #PFIL runs is therefore to cover both the possibilities of the copy to Order-out failing as well as to maintain standards of programming procedure.

The file Order-out is then dumped out by a program referred to as #XPJW to tape so that if the run fails or print-outs are lost, the file can be restored and the run repeated at a later date.

The file Order-out to which the data was output and the work file containing the end record are then sorted together into suitable sequence for print programs, i.e. into sales desk sequence (*see* **24**).

16. Customer documentation—program # OM03. The first documentation to be produced is the customer documentation which has already been mentioned above (*see* **13**). This is produced by a program referred to as #OM03 (*see* Fig. 37). This program begins by printing a list of all the orders and whether they are amended, deleted or inserted in this run. This is achieved by setting bit 20 (as a program switch) in the program. The program is then re-run with bit 23 set and the acknowledgments are then produced.

The program is run a third time with bit 22 set and this causes the order amendments to be produced (*see* Fig. 37). If stationery for order amendments is not available they can be produced on acknowledgment stationery with all the amendment notation by loading the program and setting both bit 18 and bit 22. If this situation should arise the programming section should be asked to make the necessary amendments.

The above details in respect of bit setting are summarised in Table X.

17. Works documentation—program # OM04. The next documentation to be produced is works documentation by a program

TABLE X. "BIT" SETTING: CUSTOMER DOCUMENTATION

Bit (program switch)	Print-out
20	List of orders processed
22	Order amendments
23	Acknowledgments
18 + 22	Order amendments produced on acknowledgment stationery

referred to as #OMØ4 (*see* Fig. 40). The program is first loaded with bit 23 set and this causes a list of bandas to be printed followed by the individual card bandas. The card bandas are used by the sales office to record dispatches.

The program is then loaded with bit 19 and 23 set and the documentation produced is the same as the first run but this time the bandas are printed on paper, not card, and the price is not shown because these documents will go to the mill. Bandas are produced for all bars and sections and also for plates for the present rolling week.

The term "rolling week" refers to the number of the week in which the order will be rolled and this is used to ensure that the correct documentation is produced during a batch run. The rolling week is changed every time a weekly banda and planning copy run has been done.

The program is run once more but this time bit 22 is set to enable the planning copies and list of planning copies to be produced. Planning copies are only produced for plate orders for the present rolling week.

The above details in respect of bit setting are summarised in Table XI.

18. Calculation of order value. The Order-out file is then sorted into account number sequence and the program #CRØ1 is loaded. This program selects all new orders and forms a condensed record for output containing the order number, pointer account number and value. The pointer account number is obtained by referencing the customer master file. The value is obtained by the following calculation:

[(Price per ton + carriage rate) × item weight] + V.A.T. @ 10 per cent

TABLE XI "BIT" SETTING: WORKS DOCUMENTATION

Bit (program switch)	Print-out
22	Planning copies and list of planning copies for plate orders for present rolling-week
23	List of bandas and card bandas
19 + 23	List of bandas and bandas on paper excluding price

The output file is then sorted again into account number sequence. This is done since it is more than likely that the pointer account differs from the original account number.

19. Accounts exceeding credit limit. The program #CRØ2 is then loaded into store and the list of accounts exceeding credit limit is produced for credit control purposes. This is done by adding the values of orders for a particular customer to a field on the customer master file record and checking if the credit limit is exceeded.

If the limit is exceeded the order number and value are printed out together with the customers' balances so that the credit controller can stop the order going through the mill if he thinks this is necessary.

All the programs cause a message to be output to the console whenever a change of stationery is required. All stock order bandas are produced by the program # HISH onto the termiprinters but they are listed out by the batch programs on the list of bandas produced.

ON-LINE PLANNING

20. Position in over-all system. Although the primary purpose of this case study is to indicate the nature of on-line order processing and related accounting routines, it is considered appropriate to indicate to the reader where the planning activity fits into the system. As stated previously, a video is located in the planning office and is used to put the planning details on to orders and input cast details and planning details (*see* Fig. 33 and **4**(*e*)). Four screens are available to the planning department as follows:

    screen 1—list of screens available (*see* Figs. 44–46 and 27);
    screen 3—input of cast details (*see* 29);
    screen 4—input of piece details (*see* 30);
    screen 6—input of orders for piece marking (*see* 32).

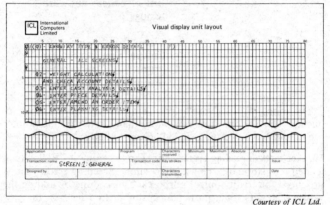

Courtesy of ICL Ltd.

FIG. 44   *Visual display unit layout: screen 1—general.*

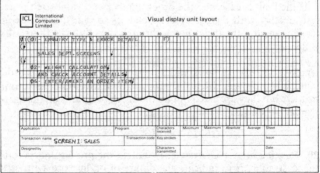

Courtesy of ICL Ltd.

FIG. 45   *Visual display unit layout: screen 1—sales.*

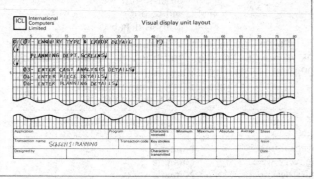

Courtesy of ICL Ltd.

FIG. 46 *Visual display unit layout: screen 1—planning.*

21. Planning files. The file V.D.U.-planning stores the data input by the videos from screens 3, 4 and 6 (*see* Fig. 33). When it is required to process the output from the planning system a message via the console causes the planning details to be copied from the Realdumpfile to the V.D.U.-planning file. The V.D.U.-planning file provides the input to the piece marking system and the Blooming Mill system (*see* Fig. 33), which are completely different systems. The details of these are beyond the scope of the present case study.

SYSTEM MASTER FILES

22. Order master. This is file 2 in the system. It serves the purpose of an on-line sales order book containing details of all outstanding orders. New orders and amendments to present orders are actioned by the on-line order entry system.

Deliveries are deleted from the file by means of the sales invoicing run (*see* **38**). Order details are updated by screen 5, and prior to the master file being updated the record is written to the dump file (realdumpfile) to facilitate the production of all batch processing routines. This is done by copying the dump file to the Order-out file once or twice a day for batch processing (*see* Fig. 33).

The order records on the master file can be accessed by screen 6 for the input of planning details (*see* **32**).

Record types contained on the file are:

Ø1—order record
99—end record
ØØ—analysis details

The file is organised on an index sequential basis with a twelve character key. The key consists of the following elements as shown in Table XII.

TABLE XII. ELEMENTS OF RECORD
KEY—ORDER MASTER RECORD

Element	Type of character	Number of characters
Order number	Numeric	5
Delivery week	Numeric	4
Sales desk	Numeric	1
Item letter	Alphabetic	1
Ø	Numeric	1

The record is 250 words long and the layout of the records is contained in the master file book. Analysis details are an integral element of the order master file.

It is necessary to reorganise the file periodically to prevent overflow areas being filled. This is done every evening by copying the file serially to a file called Order-secure and then using software to reorganise the file. This provides a security copy of the order master file as well as reorganising the file. Six generations of the file are retained.

23. Custom real. This is file 1 in the system. It serves the purpose of a customer master file containing details of customers' accounts, i.e. name and address and account balances.

Data can only be read from the file by on-line operations to facilitate validity checks on account numbers (*see* Fig. 33). Certain fields on the file are used for credit control information. The file is updated with cash and invoices at the end of the period but new account details are added as necessary during the month (*see* **41** and **45**).

The file is organised on an index sequential basis and it is necessary to reorganise the file periodically to provide for overflow conditions. For convenience this is done at the same time as the order master file.

For security purposes the file is copied to a generation of

"custom secure" and then reorganised by software. Six generations of the file are retained. The key to the file is the account number; this is six characters long. The first character of the key is alphabetic and the next five characters are numeric. The record is 250 words long. The file can be accessed by screens 2, 5 and 6. Layout of the records is contained in the master files book.

24. Order-out. This is joint file 3 in the system (*see* **26**), because both the Order-out and V.D.U.-planning file cannot be on-line to the program at the same time. Both files are made available to the system when required by means of a console directive (*see* Fig. 33).

This is the file to which order details are copied from the Real-dumpfile in readiness for batch processing of orders (*see* **15**). The file is output and the data copied to it by console message. Only records with the first two characters equal to Ø5 and the first signal equal to zero are copied (*see* Table XIII). The first two characters indicate the number of the screen from which the data originated and in this instance Ø5 refers to screen 5 which is used for entering order details by video in the sales office (*see* Fig. 33).

When a record has been written to Order-out the program will set the first bit to "one" before accessing the next record. This is done so that the record will not be output again at a later date (*see* Table XIII).

This is the file from which works and customer documentation is produced (*see* Figs. 37 and 40).

25. Realdumpfile. This is the security file of the on-line system. Any records input by video are written to this file from screen 5 (*see* Fig. 33). Before the order master file is updated the record is written to the dump file. Data is written to the file in the form of a record the first word of which is used to identify the screen from which the data was input and to decide on the processing of the record afterwards.

The first two characters contain the number of the screen from which the data came (*see* **24**). The next twelve bits identify what processing is to be done. If all twelve bits are set the record has been completely processed and can be deleted from the file (*see* Table XIII).

The bits are referred to as processing indicators which are used to keep a check on the stage processing has reached on the dump file.

TABLE XIII. "BIT" FUNCTIONS

Bit no.	Function if $= \emptyset$	Originating screen no.
$\emptyset1$	To be output to order entry batch run	$\emptyset5$
$\emptyset2$	Orders for output to screen 6	$\emptyset5$
$\emptyset3$	Orders for planning office termiprinter	$\emptyset5$
$\emptyset4$	Orders for section mill termiprinter	$\emptyset5$
$\emptyset5$ $\emptyset6$ $\emptyset7$ $\emptyset8$ $\emptyset9$ $1\emptyset$ 11	Not used, always $= 1$	
12	To be output to planning batch run	$\emptyset3, \emptyset4, \emptyset6$

26. V.D.U.-planning. This is joint file 3 in the system, as previously stated (*see* **24**). The file is used to store data input by videos from screens $\emptyset3$, $\emptyset4$ and $\emptyset6$ for use by the planning system. Data is copied to this file, following an input of a console message, from the dump file (*see* Fig. 33). Records on the dump file with the first two characters equal to $\emptyset3$ or $\emptyset4$ or $\emptyset6$ and the last signal bit equal to zero will be selected from the file. The type $\emptyset6$ records will be copied straight to the output file. Records input by screen $\emptyset3$ or screen $\emptyset4$ will be broken down into individual records and then written to the output file. This is done because the data input at any one time from this screen is written to the dump file as one record. Once the data has been copied to V.D.U.-planning the last signal (bit) is set to one so that there is no danger of the record being input on future runs. The file is then input either to the piece marking system or the mill planning system (*see* **20** and **21**, and Fig. 33).

OUTLINE OF VIDEO SCREEN AND SUB-ROUTINE FUNCTIONS

27. Screen 1. The purpose of this screen is merely to inform the video operator of the screens available and their functions. The sub-routine relevant to this screen is C002—SET1UP. This sub-routine checks the video department and on this depends the output to the screen. The field "video department" (*see* Figs. 44–46) will contain one of the characters G, S, or P. These relate to "general", "sales" and "planning". The screen output will list the screens available to the video. This is to ensure that sales screens are not used by planning.

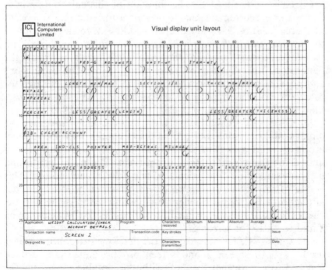

FIG. 47 *Visual display unit layout: screen 2—weight calculation/check account details.*

28. Screen 2. This screen (*see* Fig. 47), is used to check if an account number is on the file and/or calculate the weight of an order. If the error message generated is "undesirable section" refer the order to the sales desk (*see* Table XIV). If any other errors are output check that the data was correctly entered on the screen. If it was refer the order to the sales desk otherwise correct the data and resubmit. If the data has been accepted, copy the weight or number of units on to the pro-forma. There are six sub-routines to this screen, three of which are also used by screen 5.

The sub-routines are as follows:

(*a*) C003—SCRN2VAL. This sub-routine validates the account number and sets up to read the customer master file. The sub-routine is then re-entered and details of the account, if found, are placed in the message area and the control is passed across to sub-routine C004. If the account number was invalid or the account was not present on the master file an appropriate message is placed in the error message field and the next sub-routine to be called is C008 to be output to the screen.

(*b*) C004—SIZECALC. The function of this sub-routine is to convert imperial dimensions, if present, to metric and the result of the calculation is rounded up by adding .9 to the length and the section and .009 to the thickness. The plus percentage and minus percentage fields are then validated and if necessary the dimensions are adjusted by these percentages. The dimensions and product group are then placed in the additional core area for calculation of weight in future sub-routines. If there are any errors the next sub-routine called is C008 otherwise it is C005.

(*c*) C005—CHECKDIMS. This sub-routine validates the dimensions to ensure they are numeric, checks that the product group is valid and then checks that only those dimensions required for this product group are present. The mean length and mean thickness are then calculated and held in core storage. This is one of the sub-routines also called by screen 5. If all the validity checks are passed the next sub-routine called is C006. If the checks failed for any reason control is passed to C008 for screen 2 and to C026 for screen 5.

(*d*) C006—SIZEVAL. As with the previous sub-routine, this is used by both screen 2 and screen 5. The dimensions are all checked to ensure that they are within acceptable ranges for the particular product group. If there are errors in the data the next sub-routine called is either C008 for screen 2 or C026 for screen

TABLE XIV. SCREEN 2 ERROR MESSAGES

Error Message	Reason and Action
ACCOUNT NO. NOT ON FILE	The account no. requested is not on the computer files. Return enquiry to the sales desk and ask them to make a master file amendment.
INVALID ACCOUNT NO.	The account no. requested does not (a) have an alpha character first or (b) have five numeric characters after the alpha. Re-enter and send again.
INVALID IMPERIAL FORMAT	The solidii are missing from the imperial dimensions. Re-enter and send again.
PERCENTAGE INVALID	The plus/minus per cent fields are not numeric. Re-enter and send again.
NON-NUMERIC LENGTH	The field contains non-numeric characters.
NON-NUMERIC WIDTH	
NON-NUMERIC THICKNESS	Re-enter and send again.
UNDESIRABLE SECTION	The section for product group 1 is less than 280mm. The weight will have been calculated. Refer the order to the desk.
INVALID NO-UNITS	No. of units not numeric correct and send again.
INVALID PRODUCT GROUP	The product group given is not in the range 1 to 8. Correct and send again.
MAXIMUM LENGTH PRESENT	Minimum length only is allowed for product groups 1 and 2. Correct and send again.
SECOND SECTION PRESENT	Only product group 3 is allowed to have a second section. Correct and send again.
MAX. THICKNESS PRESENT	Maximum thickness is not allowed for product groups 3, 4, 5 or 6. Correct and send again.
FIRST SECTION PRESENT	The first section is not allowed for product groups 5 and 8. Correct and send again.

TABLE XIV.—*contd.*

Error Message	Reason and Action
LENGTH MAX. NOT. MIN.	The maximum length of bar has been put in shorter than the minimum length. Correct and send again.
THICK. MAX. NOT MIN.	The maximum thickness of plates has been put in thinner than the minimum thickness of plates. Correct and send again.
INVALID LENGTH	The length given is greater than the mills can roll. Return the order to the sales desk.
INVALID WIDTH	The width of the plate is greater or less than the mill can handle. Return to sales desk.
INVALID THICKNESS	The thickness of the plate is greater or less than the mill can handle. Return the order to the sales desk.
INVALID SECTION	The section of bar given is not in the mill product range. Return the order to the sales desk.

5. If the data was correct the next sub-routine is C007.

(*e*) C007—WEIGHTCALC. Once again this sub-routine is used by both screen 2 and 5. Its function is to calculate the unit weight of an order. The weight calculation is different for each product group (P.G.).

P.G.1. = MEAN-LENGTH * MEAN-THICK * SECT-1 * 0.00785

P.G.3. = Search table for section and thickness to give constant.
Result = CONSTANT * MEAN-LENGTH

P.G.4. = Adjust section and thickness by finding the equivalent in the table. The actual calculation is as for P.G.1.

P.G.5. = Adjust the thickness for greater accuracy.
MEAN-LENGTH * MEAN-THICK * ADJ-THICK * 0.00785

There is no unit weight calculation for P.G.2, 6 and 7. Once the unit weight is calculated either the no-units is worked out by dividing the item weight by the unit weight and adding one to the result, or else the item weight is calculated by multiplying the unit weight by the no-units.

As this sub-routine is used by both screen 2 and screen 5 the next sub-routine to be called is either CØØ8 or CØ23.

(f) CØØ8—SET2UP. This sub-routine forms the data in the message area into an acceptable format for output to the video.

29. Screen 3. This screen is used by the planning office for the input of cast analysis details to the piece marking system. There are up to ten sets of data input per screen and this data is used to update the analysis file by a batch run. When the data has been accepted a "blank" screen is returned. Sub-routines concerned with this screen are omitted as they are beyond the scope of this case study.

30. Screen 4. This screen is a planning department screen and is used for the input of piece details for input to the piece marking system. When the data is accepted by the computer a "blank" screen is returned.

Sub-routines concerned with this screen are omitted as they are beyond the scope of this case study.

31. Screen 5. This screen is used to update the order master file. If the order to be inserted on the file is one that was reported as being undesirable by screen 2 it is necessary to type the word ACCEPT in the error message area in order to add it to the file. For an ordinary insertion the error message is left blank. For an amendment or deletion the order item number and amend code are keyed in first and sent to the computer. On return the screen will contain all details of the order as held on the file.

The amendment is then done and to action this the word AMENDED is typed into the error message field prior to transmitting the data. If the order is to be deleted the word DELETE is entered into this field.

If a planning copy has been produced for an amendment or deletion the words P/COPY PRODUCED will have been output to the message area when the order was presented on the screen. It is most important that the appropriate sales desk be informed of this so that they can stop the progress of this order through the mill.

Sub-routines concerned with this screen are as follows:

(a) CØ21—SCRN5VAL1. This sub-routine validates the order number and amend type. Amend types include (1) insertion, (2) amendment and (3) deletion.

If the error message field is = AMEND or DELETE the rest of the screen is validated. If the amend type is equal to (2) or (3) and the error message is equal to spaces, sub-routine CØ24 is the next to be called. If there are no errors in the data the next sub-routine to be called is CØ22 otherwise control is passed to CØ26.

(b) CØ22—SCRN5VAL2. The function of this sub-routine is to validate the remainder of the screen. If the data is correct and the order is for product group 2, 6 or 7 (see **28**(e)), the next sub-routine called is CØ23. If the data is invalid control is passed to CØØ5, which is part of screen 2 (see **28**), and if there are errors the next sub-routine to be called is CØ26.

(c) CØ23—FORMREC. This sub-routine will check that an order for amendment or deletion is present on the master file and that an insertion is not present. If either of these checks fail, the next sub-routine to be called will be CØ26. The record is formed in the input/output area if it has satisfied the checks and is set up to be written to the dump file, and this sub-routine is re-entered. On re-entry the record is either written to, amended on or deleted from the order master file and sub-routine CØ26 is called.

(d) CØ24—FORMSCRN1. The function of this sub-routine is to put the data from the record read off the master file into the message area and the key is set up to look for the name and address. If the order has not been found the next sub-routine to be called is CØ26 otherwise control is passed to CØ25.

(e) CØ25—FORMSCRN2. This sub-routine will put the name and address from the customer master file record into the message area.

(f) CØ26—SET5UP. The purpose of this sub-routine is to re-format the message area into a suitable format for output to the video (see Fig. 48 and Table XV).

32. Screen 6. This screen allows the planning office to access an order on the master file by entering the order number. This will cause the order to be presented on the screen together with analysis details if found. If it is required to override the computer analysis details enter the new details and type in the message ACCEPT ANALYSIS in the field where error messages are output.

The security system allows orders to be output to the video by the operator typing in the word NEXT in the error message field. If the analysis details are changed on this part of the system the message to be keyed in is ACCEPT NEXT. This part of the system is only to be used after checking with the computer department. Sub-routines concerned with this screen are omitted as they are beyond the scope of this case study.

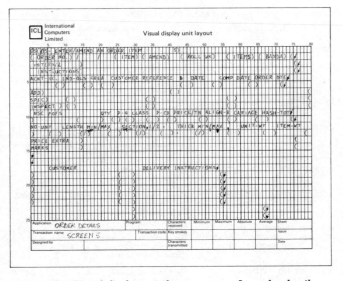

FIG. 48 *Visual display unit layout: screen 5—order details.*

TABLE XV. SCREEN 5 ERROR MESSAGES

Error Message	Reason and Action
MAXIMUM LENGTH PRESENT SECOND SECTION PRESENT INVALID PRODUCT GROUP MAX. THICKNESS PRESENT FIRST SECTION PRESENT LENGTH MAX. NOT MIN. THICK. MAX. NOT MIN. INVALID LENGTH INVALID WIDTH INVALID THICKNESS INVALID SECTION NON-NUMERIC LENGTH NON-NUMERIC WIDTH NON-NUMERIC THICKNESS INVALID NO-UNITS	Error details as for screen 2.
INVALID UNIT-WT	The unit weight given is invalid for the sizes given. Check the coding and if necessary use screen 2 to re-calculate weight.
INVALID ITEM-WT	The item weight given is invalid for the no. of units given. Check the coding and if necessary use screen 2 to re-calculate weight.

TABLE XV.—*contd.*

Error Message	Reason and Action
INVALID ORDER/ITEM NO.	The order no. given is invalid (the sales desk must be in range 1 to 4, the order part greater than ∅ and the delivery week in range 1 to 53). The item no. given is not in the range A to Z. Correct and send again.
INVALID COMPLETION DATE	Either the date is not valid or it is not proceeded by B or N. Correct and send again.
INVALID ACCOUNT NO.	The letter of the account no. is not in the range A to Z or the first three numbers are not in the range 1 to 998 or the last two numbers are not in the range 1 to 98. Correct and send again.
INVALID CUSTOMER DATE	The customer's date is not a valid date. Correct and send again.
INVALID DETAIL SIGNAL	The signals for computer, additional process, specification and inspection are not Y or N. Correct and send again.
INVALID AMEND CODE (COVERS PRICE CHANGES AND REVISED DELIVERY DATE, ETC.)	The amend code not in range 1 to 3. The amendment type letter is not in range A to Z or wrong code for deletion (*see* sub-routine C∅ 21). Correct and send again.
ACCOUNT NO. NOT ON FILE	The account no. given is not on the master file. Return to the sales desk for a master file amendment to be made.
NO NO-UNITS	No no. of units has been given. Correct and send again.
ORDER ALREADY ON FILE	The order/item you are trying to amend is already on the orders file. Check coding and return order to sales desk.
NO ORDER TO AMEND/DELETE	The order/item you are trying to amend or delete is not on the order file. Check coding and return to the sales desk.
INVALID BEFORE/AFTER	The before/after signal is not = B or N or A. Correct and send again.
INVALID ROLL WEEK	Roll week = STOC and first character of order No. not = ∅. Roll week not numeric or out of range 1 to 53. Correct and send again.
ROLL > DELIVERY	Roll week >delivery week. Correct and send again.
INVALID BANDA	Banda not = Y or N. Correct and send again.
INVALID ORDER DATE	The order date is not a valid date. Correct and send again.
INVALID LAST ITEM	Items letter A or Z. Correct and send again.

TABLE XV.—*contd.*

Error Message	Reason and Action
INVALID SPECIFICATION	Specification code not in acceptable range. Correct and send again.
INVALID NO-TESTS	No-tests not numeric. Correct and send again.
INVALID PROCESS SIGNALS	Process signals not = Y or N. Correct and send again.
INVALID PRICE CODE	Price code = 7 or less than 1 or greater than 8. Correct and send again.
INVALID ALIGN RATE	Align rate present for price code 1, 2, 3, 6 or 8 not present for price code 4, 5. Correct and send again.
INVALID AREA	Area invalid. Correct and send again.
INVALID SYMBOL	Symbol invalid. Correct and send again.
HASH TOTAL DISAGREES	Total price entered incorrectly. Correct and send again.
UNDESIRABLE SECTION	The section is of undesirable proportions; check with the sales desk if it is to be input. If it is, type ACCEPT in the error message and send again. If the order is an amendment, it will have to be cancelled and re-issued.

33. Other sub-routines.

(*a*) CØØØ—ERRORRECOV. This sub-routine is called when an error occurs. Its function is to check the error, if "known" error occurs sub-routine CØ13 is called otherwise the request area is printed out on the console.

(*b*) CØ13—PMRECOV. This sub-routine will display an error message on the console and cause screen 1 to be output to the video.

(*c*) CØ15—INITIALISE. The function of this sub-routine is to open all the devices and files that are attached to the system. This is done by the sub-routine re-entering itself.

34. Message Processing.
This is the name given to the group of sub-routines which process the messages input by console.

(*a*) CØ16—MESSPATH. If the first word of the console message is OUTPUT, control is passed across to CØ17. Sub-routine CØ18 is called if the message is INPUT and sub-routine CØ2Ø is called for a SYSTEM message. The messages to open and close files, and to switch terminals on and off are processed by this sub-routine by allowing re-entry into the sub-routine.

(b) CØ17—OUTMESS. This sub-routine first of all opens the output file to which data is to be written. This file is either Order-out or V.D.U.-planning. The sub-routine is then re-entered and it proceeds to scan the dump file to pick up the next order for output. If the order is to be output the record is written back to the dump file signalled as being output. The sub-routine is re-entered and the record written to the output file and the sub-routine set up to be re-entered once again. This re-entry will cause the Dump file to be searched for the next record.

The records for output are identified by the first word of the record on the Dump file. The first two characters identify the screen number from which the record was formed and thus are used to determine which file they are to be output to. Records containing Ø5 will be output to Order-out. Those containing Ø3, Ø4 or Ø6 will be output to V.D.U.-planning. The next twelve bits of the word are used to signal whether the record has been pro-cessed or is awaiting processing and what type of processing is to take place (*see* **24, 26** and Table XIII).

(c) CØ18—INMESS. This sub-routine is used to copy orders for a specific planning week from the order master file to the dump file for use by screen 6. This is done by the use of re-entry of the sub-routine.

(d) CØ19—FILETIDY. This sub-routine is called whenever orders have been output from the dump file. Its function is to delete all the records that have been completely processed from the dump file so that the file will contain only records awaiting output.

(e) CØ2Ø—SYSTMESS. The function of this sub-routine is to process the system messages.

VIDEO OPERATING INSTRUCTIONS

The following details should be studied in conjunction with Fig. 49.

35. Switching on procedure.

(a) Switch the power on at mains.

(b) Switch on video using on/off switch on the front of the video. The "system ready" and "type" lights will now be illumi-nated if the video is on-line to the computer.

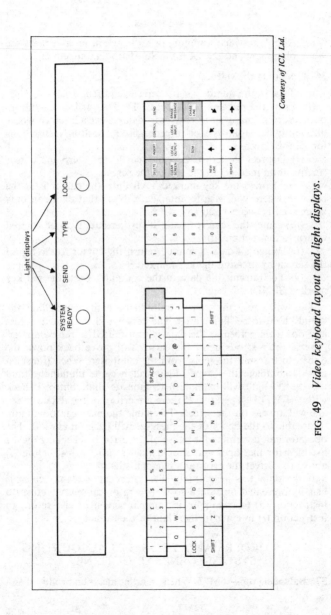

FIG. 49 *Video keyboard layout and light displays.*

Courtesy of ICL Ltd.

(*c*) Allow the video a minute or so to warm up and press the white blank key and the CLEAR SCREEN key together.

36. Operating the video.

(*a*) Type in the number of the screen required.

(*b*) Press the red key marked SEND. This will cause the required screen to appear after a short delay. As each screen works differently here follows a set of generalised operating instructions for all the screens.

(*i*) Depress the green key marked ↖ to return the cursor (the position marker) to the top of the screen.

(*ii*) Depress the key marked TAB until the cursor is at the position where you wish to enter data. Note that data can only be entered between) and (.

(*iii*) Enter the required data. If further data is to be entered return to instruction (*ii*).

(*iv*) When all data is entered return the cursor to the top of the screen by pressing the key marked ↖ .

(*v*) To transmit the data to the computer press the red key marked SEND.

This will cause the "type" light to be extinguished and the "send" light to be illuminated. The cursor will then move across and down the screen as the data is transmitted to the computer. After a few seconds delay the cursor will move back down the screen to transmit the reply from the computer. When transmission is complete the "type" light will become illuminated and the "send" light will extinguish to indicate that control is back with the V.D.U. operator. If there are errors in the data a message will appear on the screen. To enable the message to be more noticeable to the operator the message will flash on and off. The operator can determine the cause of the error by checking on the list of error messages and should then return to instruction (*i*) above to correct the error and resubmit the data.

If the data was accepted by the computer a blank screen is usually presented on return so the operator can either return to instruction (*a*) to change to a different screen or else return to instruction (*i*) to enter further data of the same type.

SALES ORDERS AND THE SALES ACCOUNTING SYSTEM—GENERAL OUTLINE

37. Balancing run— ∅M73. When an order has been produced and delivered to the customer, a document known as an invoice production copy (I.P.C.) is sent from the planning department to the sales office. This document is a photocopy of the banda with a box on the bottom for recording delivery details (*see* Fig. 42). These details are used to update the order record cards in the sales office with the number of units and weight delivered.

The I.P.C.s are batched and sent to the computer department. The details are punched into cards and input to a validation and balancing run (*see* Fig. 50). Invalid details are printed out on an error listing. Valid details are recorded on work-file 1 which is input to the invoicing run when all the batches balance.

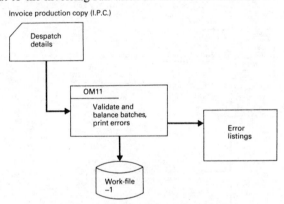

Invoice production copy (I.P.C.)

FIG. 50 *Flowchart: invoicing—balancing run.*

38. Invoicing runs—ØM74. Referring to Fig. 51 it can be seen that the first run is concerned with sorting work-file 1 containing valid I.P.C. details into record type within account number by I.P.C. number. The sorted I.P.C.s are recorded on work-file 2 which is input to ØM05. In this run details of I.P.C.s are input and checked against the order master file, which is the sales order book, to ensure there is an order present on the file. Dispatches are validated and the order master file is updated with deliveries. Errors are printed out on an error report. The weight of dispatches are also printed on a weight report. It is important to appreciate that the order master file is closed to the on-line system during these stages of processing.

Details on work-file 1 are dumped to magnetic tape to allow a re-run if necessary. Orders that are correct are then invoiced and

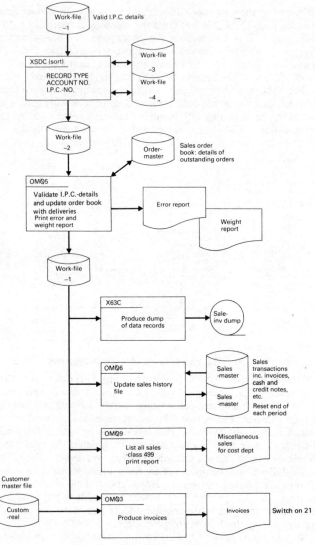

FIG. 51 *Flowchart: invoicing runs.*

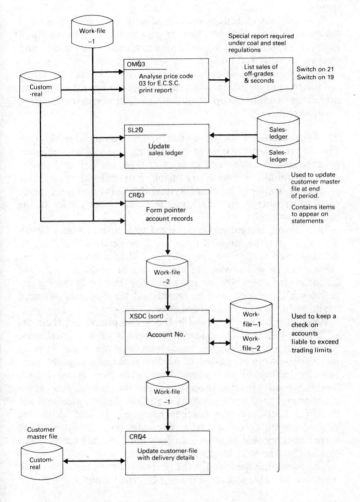

FIG. 51—*contd.*

the order and invoice details are then updated on the sales master file. The file is a cumulative monthly file for sales history requirements.

A further set of runs is concerned with the production of a summary of miscellaneous sales for the cost office, the printing of invoices, production of a special report required under coal and steel regulations and updating the sales ledger file.

In addition, routines embracing runs CRØ3, XSDC and CRØ4 are for the purpose of maintaining a check on accounts liable to exceed credit limits and updating delivery details on customer file—Custom-real.

39. Miscellaneous sales items—ØM79. This routine is outlined in Fig. 52. It is not possible to produce all invoices by computer because certain sales, such as sales of slag, are not held on the order master file. It is necessary therefore to deal with these transactions by a manual invoicing system. It is also necessary, however, to provide input details of the value of such sales to the computer system.

In addition, certain goods delivered to a customer may be defective, or may be invoiced incorrectly, or perhaps could not be delivered and will have to be redispatched at a later date. These circumstances will necessitate the issuing of credit notes to the customer for the value of the materials. In the case of a redelivery a credit note will be issued and the customer invoiced again when the goods are redelivered.

Items may have been placed in the wrong period and these are adjusted by the credit controller by means of a journal item. These journals, credit notes, miscellaneous invoices and cash received details are all passed through a series of computer runs. Initially, the input data is copied from cards to magnetic disc (to facilitate more effective processing) and then sorted into batch number and card code key-field sequence. The transactions are then validated and the batches balanced. Invalid items are printed out on an error report. The valid transactions are then sorted into account number sequence and updated on the sales master file. The sales ledger is also updated.

The remaining runs are for the purpose of maintaining a check on accounts liable to exceed trading or credit limits.

40. Credit control balances—ØM82. This routine is outlined in Fig. 53. Outstanding orders for a specific week are selected from

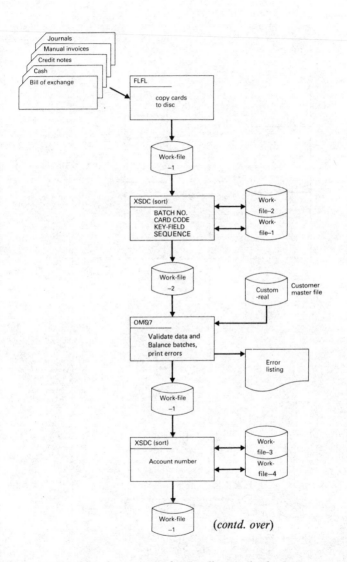

FIG. 52 *Flowchart: input of "miscellaneous" sales items.*

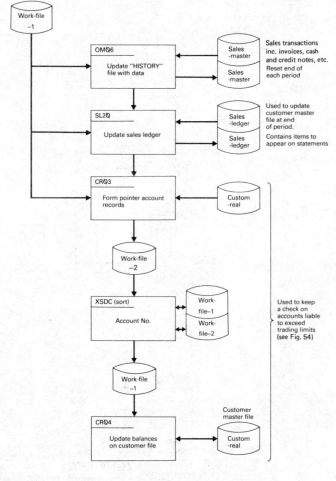

FIG. 52—*contd.*

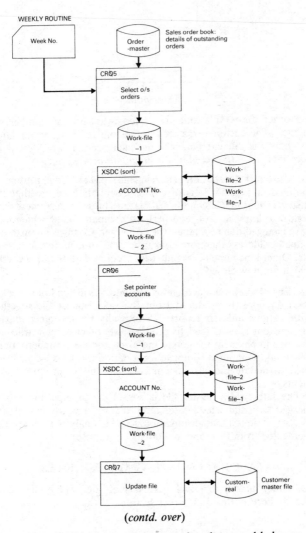

(*contd. over*)

FIG. 53 *Flowchart: calculation of credit control balances.*

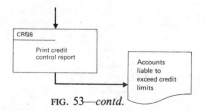

FIG. 53—*contd.*

the order master file and are sorted into account number sequence. The customer master file (custom real) is then updated to show the current balances on each account and details of accounts liable to exceed credit limits are printed out.

41. Customer master file amendments—0M84. This routine is outlined in Fig. 54. It is of course essential to ensure that the customer master file contains the latest status of customers with regard to latest address and perhaps company name which may have changed due to a take-over or merger. Changes of customer name or address therefore constitute amendments to the master file. Other amendments include new account details and accounts which are now closed.

42. End of week sales accounting routines. At the end of a week a sales daybook is produced from the sales master file together with various analysis reports. Periodically the customer master file (custom real) is read to produce lists of customers who are overdue in payment for goods and also produce reminder letters. When all the input is complete for a period the sales ledger file is used to update the customer master file and to produce statements.

The latest sales master file is sorted on to tape and this is merged with the sales master tape to form a yearly cumulative file. At various times throughout the year analysis runs are implemented from this tape for statistical purposes.

SALES ACCOUNTING MASTER FILES

43. Order master file and custom real file. These files have already been outlined in earlier sections of the book (*see* **22** and **23**).

44. Sales master. This file, as well as containing details of completed orders, also contains details of all invoices (both computer

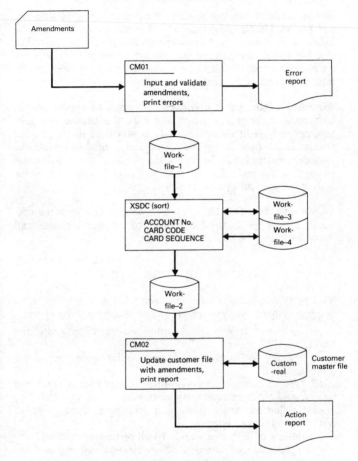

FIG. 54 *Flowchart: customer master file amendments.*

produced and manually produced), cash, credit notes, journals and bills of exchange. The sales master file which is held on disc is a cumulative file for the present period. At the end of the period the data on the disc file is copied to a tape called "sales month" and the disc file is reset to allow input of data for the next period. The tape file is used to allow the production of the sales statistics and at the same time not to delay the processing of data for the new period. The file "sales month" is then merged with the tape file called "sales master" to form a cumulative file for the year. The disc file is reset at the end of each period by use of PFIL to input an end record to the file. This is also done on the sales master tape at the end of the year.

45. Sales ledger. This file contains all items to appear on the customers' statements, i.e. cash and bills of exchange, journals, invoices and credit notes. The data is added to the file by the various batch runs during the period and is used to update the customer master file at the end of the period. The file is dumped to tape at the end of each week to facilitate recovery of the system in the event of a breakdown.

46. Overdue file. This file is used in conjunction with the customer master file to produce details of overdue accounts and reminder letters for the credit controller.

OVERVIEW OF CASE STUDY IV

This is to enable the reader to check what has been learnt of systems design from this case study and as a basis for review:

(*a*) outline of application regarding on-line order processing and related sub-systems;

(*b*) reasons for converting to an on-line order processing system;

(*c*) type of computer configuration required for a combined on-line and batch processing application;

(*d*) outline of order processing routine including use of V.D.U.s and termiprinters;

(*e*) outline of daily and weekly batch processing routines;

(*f*) production of customer documentation and works documentation including "bit" setting for program switches;

(*g*) procedure for accounts exceeding credit limit;

(*h*) on-line planning and its position in the system;

(*i*) the nature of on-line file requirements in the system either for updating or reference purposes including the structure of record keys;

(*j*) nature and purpose of V.D.U. screens and sub-routines;

(*k*) procedure for dealing with error messages;

(*l*) outline of video operating instructions;

(*m*) video keyboard layout;

(*n*) sales accounting routines including file amendments and the nature of sales accounting master files.

Food Wholesaling: On-line Order Processing

GENERAL CONSIDERATIONS

1. Company profile. This case study relates to the operations of a traditional food wholesaling business wishing to remain anonymous. Although the name of the company is not disclosed, purely for matters of policy, the reader need not be concerned with the lack of corporate identity as this does not in any way affect the value of the details which follow.

The company supplies a large commodity range consisting of 10,000 lines to a large number of retailers (approximately 1,000) from each of ten depots. Each depot handles 6,000 order lines each day and the policy of the business is to achieve same day loading of order lines with a twenty-four hour turnround. This is a very demanding schedule to maintain. The depots are dispersed throughout the country as a consequence of various mergers and take-overs. Each depot receives in the region of 3,000–4,000 orders each month. The number of line items per order varies between an average of 40 and a maximum of 700.

Some of the depots operate clerical order processing systems and others are operating punched card equipment which, as well as being obsolete, is not capable of achieving the requirements of the business. The number of orders received from customers is increasing continuously and an efficient method of processing orders is required at each of the depots. The company has already considered the implementation of decentralised computer systems at each of the depots operating in batch processing mode but has rejected this type of processing because of its inflexibility, cost and failure to meet system objectives. The company has also come to the conclusion that a high-powered centralised computer system operating in batch or on-line mode would either be too cumbersome with regard to batch processing or too ambitious, at present, in respect of centralised on-line processing. The circumstances tend to indicate a need for decentralised on-line order processing using a small interactive computer system at each of the depots.

P.L.O.F. – PRICE LIST ORDER FORM

1	Retail Price	Cost	Qty Wk 1	Code	Qty Wk 2
100/Asstd. Licorice				086977	
50/Oodles				086979	
200/Supadoops				086981	
100/Licorice Ropes				086983	
200/Bubbly				086985	
150/Blackeye				086987	
100/Fruity Snips				086989	
30/Sportsman				086991	
60/XL Fruit				086993	
24/Spearmint				086...	
24/Everton Mints				086073	
24/Choc Eclairs				086092	
24/Orange & Lemon				086089	
24/Mint Imps				086085	
24/Soft Cent Fruits				086093	
24/Crystal Fruits				086069	
24/Nut Brittle				086079	
5lb L.L.V. Loz				086139	
24/L.L.V. Loz Bag				086094	
24/V.V. Gums Bag				086095	
24/L.L.V. Loz Tube				086137	
24/V.V. Gum Tube				086141	

2	Retail Price	Cost	Qty Wk 1	Code	Qty Wk 2
5½lb/Princess Almonds				086065	
4½lb/Choc Eclairs				086045	
5lb/Orange & Lemon Slices				086059	
5lb/Everton Mints				086053	
4lb/Nut Brittle				086057	
5lb/Crystal Fruits				086049	
5lb/Barley Sugar				086041	
4½lb/Chewy Mints				086047	
4lb/Soft Centre Fruits				086055	
Raisins				086061	
Seafood					
150/World of Sport				086221	
144/Lic. Telephones				086222	
150/Squeakers				086223	
150/Gobstoppers				086224	
100/Jollypops				086225	
100/Giant Gobstoppers				086226	
120/Sherbet Chews				086227	
120/Banana Chews				086060	
120/Caramel Chews				086051	
120/Milk Chews				086052	
120/Lemon Chews				086053	
120/Spearmint Chews				086054	

3	Retail Price	Cost	Qty Wk 1	Code	Qty Wk 2
120/Raspberry Chews				088055	
120/Pineapple Chews				088056	
120/Liquorice Chews				088057	
120/Orange Chews				088058	
72/Whoppa Stopper Pkts				086228	
72/Comforters				085199	
72/Devils				086209	
72/Chessmen				086229	
72/Sweet Bananas					
gowatch				203	
48/...				247	
7lb/Sherbet...				086248	
7lb/Tom Thumb Drops				086249	

FIG. 55 Price list order form (P.L.O.F.).

Pre-printed price list order forms (P.L.O.F.) (*see* Fig. 55), are used throughout the group and management have decided to retain the existing line code numbers even though they do not contain check digits. The system need not therefore provide for check digit verification. Stocks are controlled at present by stock records maintained by clerical procedures. Future developments will no doubt embrace full stock control.

Credit authorisations are at present handled by clerical methods; management consider the present procedure suitable for the needs of the business and do not contemplate computerising credit control. The posting of the sales ledger is also a clerical operation.

2. Considerations of proposed system. The main requirements of the on-line order processing system includes provision for the following:

(*a*) order entry routine whereby details of orders are input by means of a V.D.U.;

(*b*) preparation of order picking lists;

(*c*) order amendment routine whereby amendments are entered by means of a V.D.U.;

(*d*) preparation of business documents including invoices, credit notes and statements;

(*e*) generation of file security copies;

(*f*) printing of retail sales ledger and catering sales ledger reports;

(*g*) printing of gross margin report;

(*h*) processing transaction deletions;

(*i*) printing of representatives' product sales analysis, customer product sales analysis and product sales analysis;

(*j*) listing of consortium case sales, product case sales and customer profile data;

(*k*) monthly and year-end resetting of files, i.e. customer, product and sales history files;

(*l*) listing of products on contract showing prices and list of customers on contract;

(*m*) listing of all customers by ledger prefix;

(*n*) listing of product file showing prices and margins.

The block diagram illustrated in Fig. 56 broadly indicates the above requirements.

GENERAL STRUCTURE OF THE SYSTEM

3. Computer configuration. The small interactive computer system implemented at each of the depots is the I.C.L. System Ten (formerly the Singer System Ten) which is one of the most cost effective computer systems available. It is a totally modular computer which may be used for both batch and on-line operations concurrently. For on-line or real-time requirements the system provides a fast response to requests for information and processing requirements. Up to twenty requests can be dealt with simultaneously on an interactive basis. The configuration consists of:

(*a*) central processor with a memory capacity of 60 K characters;

(*b*) three V.D.U.s (varies according to needs of individual depots);

(*c*) one work station;

(*d*) one line printer;

(*e*) two disc drives.

4. System input. The primary input to the order processing system is provided by a pre-printed price list order form (P.L.O.F.) (*see* Fig. 55). Details from these documents are input by means of a V.D.U. including:

(*a*) account number;

(*b*) order number;

(*c*) product code;

(*d*) quantity.

The details of each order are stored on an orders file on disc (*see* **38**).

5. Files. The main files used in the system are outlined below:

(*a*) orders file;

(*b*) customer file;

(*c*) product file;

(*d*) product classification file;

(*e*) contract file;

(*f*) sales history file;

(*g*) representatives' name file.

6. System output. Details of the output produced by the various processing routines are listed in Table XVI and shown on Fig. 56.

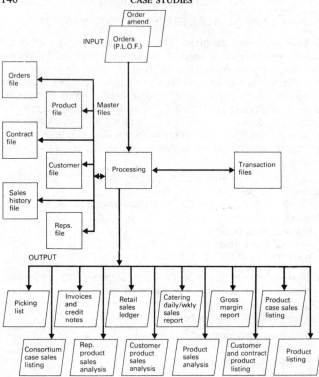

FIG. 56 *Block diagram showing structure of on-line order entry system.*

7. Processing routines. The various processing routines are indicated in Table XVI and outlined in various flowcharts throughout the book.

8. Customer types. The customer file contains a data element "customer type"; this is because food wholesaling operations normally have different types of customer and those relevant to this particular business are classified as follows.

    01: Contract caterer.
    02: Consortium.
    10: Free-Trade caterer.
    21: Alliance of Private traders (A.P.T.) full member.
    26: Alliance of Private traders (A.P.T.) associate member.

39: C.T.N. (confectionary, tobacco, newsagents' shop).
99: Frozen food—C.O.D.

9. Wholesale price factor. The product file contains a data element "wholesale price factor" which is used for calculating invoice line extensions as follows:

$$\frac{\text{quantity or weight} \times \text{price}}{\text{wholesale price factor}}$$

10. Commodity location codes. The product file contains a data element "location code". The relevant codes are listed below.

000: General warehouse.	T00: Tobacco room.
B00: Bacon room.	Z00: Splits.
C00: Cheese room.	–S–: Direct sugar.
M00: Wines and spirits.	F00: Frozen food.

11. Bulkmark. The product file contains a code ("bulkmark") which indicates to the order entry program the type of entry required.

The relevant codes used for the purpose are listed below.

0: Quantity only.
1: Quantity, processing instruction and weight (refers to bacon or cheese, i.e. bulk items).
2: Quantity and weight.

12. Transaction types. The types of transactions which the system is designed to handle are listed below.

(1) Main order. A retail P.L.O.F. or any catering order causes a retail statement to be produced. The price is obtained from the product file.

(2) Retail supplementary. Details summarised and stored for the preparation of a retail statement. Price obtained from the product file.

(3) Credit note. Details summarised and stored for the preparation of a retail statement if for a retailer. Price obtained from the product file.

(4) Drop shipment. Details summarised and stored for a retail statement if for a retailer. The price is entered through the keyboard.

(5) Credit note. Details summarised and stored for the preparation of a retail statement if for a retailer. Price entered through the keyboard.

(6) Frozen food. Details summarised and stored for the preparation of a retail statement if for a retailer. Price obtained from the product file.

(7) Retail confectionery. Details summarised and stored for the preparation of a retail statement. Price obtained from the product file.

13. Pricing. Prices of products for various customer types (*see* **8**) are stored on the product file or contract file. Discounts allowed off the price of various product groups and off the invoice are stored on the customer file. All prices are taken into account at the time of order entry. *See* order-entry (VDORDS) routine, Fig. 59. The pricing structure is outlined below.

(*a*) Retail customer (types 21 and over);
   (*i*) retail price from the product file if not zero;
   (*ii*) catering price from the product file.

(*b*) Free-trade caterer (type 10 only):
   (*i*) catering price from the product file if not zero;
   (*ii*) retail price from the product file plus 5 per cent.

(*c*) Contract caterer (types 01 and 02):
   (*i*) special price for a particular product from the contract file;
   (*ii*) catering price from the product file, plus or minus the percentage held in the contract file;
   (*iii*) retail price from the product file plus 5 per cent, plus or minus the percentage held in the contract file;
   (*iv*) catering price from the product file, plus or minus the percentage held in the customer file;
   (*v*) retail price from the product file plus 5 per cent, plus or minus the percentage held in the customer file;
   (*vi*) catering price from the product file;
   (*vii*) retail price from the product file plus 5 per cent.

14. Calculation of retail margin. The calculation is based on the following formula.

$$\frac{(\text{No. of retail units} \times \text{R.R.S.P.}) - (\text{Selling price} + \text{V.A.T.})}{(\text{No. of retail units} \times \text{R.R.S.P.})} \times 100$$

Any one factor being incorrect will produce wrong information on the invoice.

15. Discounts off invoice. A discount indicator is an element contained in the product file, "1" indicates that a discount is relevant and "0" indicates that a discount is not relevant. Other discount factors are contained in the customer file (*see* **39**). The discount structure and rules applicable to specific types of customer are outlined below.

(*a*) Retail customer. A standard scale of discounts is held in the invoicing program for all retailers. The total turnover since last main order is added to the value of the current main order to determine the discount percentage to be given (*see* customer master file, **39**). If not a main order, the value of the invoice only is used. This system will be bypassed if a fixed discount is found in the customer file. A separate scale of discounts is held for retail confectionery transaction type 7 (*see* **12**). V.A.T. is calculated after discount is given. Discount is calculated on discountable goods only.

(*b*) Free-trade catering. A standard scale of discounts is held in the invoicing program for all caterers. The value of the invoice is used to determine the discount percentage to be given. This system will be bypassed if a fixed discount is found in the customer file. V.A.T. is calculated after discount is given. Discount is calculated on discountable goods only.

(*c*) Contract catering. There is only one discount provision available to contract catering. This is determined by checking the discount off the invoice field in the customer file (*see* **39**). This discount is given off all products if the minimum value has been attained (*see* customer file, **39**). V.A.T. is calculated after discount is given.

16. V.A.T. codes. The appropriate code determines the rate of tax applicable to an item. The actual percentage is held in the program. The structure of tax codes are listed below.

W—zero rated.
R—standard rate (at present 15 per cent).
Y—spare.
B—spare.

PROCESSING ROUTINES

17. Program names. Each processing routine is allocated a program name for identification purposes. Table XVI indicates these names together with the frequency with which such routines are performed. The relevant program names facilitate reference to the flowchart outlining the basic processing features of each routine. Each flowchart is headed with its program name.

TABLE XVI. SUMMARY OF PROCESSING ROUTINES

Routine	Program name	Frequency of routine			
		End of day	End of week	End of period	End of year
Order entry	VDORDS				
Picking lists	PICK				
Order amend	VDORAM	On-line operations			
Invoice and credit note production	INVOIC/CREDIT				
Security copies	SECURE-COPYD	×	×	×	×
Retail sales ledger	RETAIL INC.				
	RETLEG	—	×	×	×
Catering sales ledger: daily/weekly sales report	ACT INC. INVLST	×	×	×	×
Daily gross margin report	ORESET	×	×	×	×
Transaction file 2 deletions	TR2DEL	×	×	×	×
Representatives product sales analysis	SALES 3 INC.				
	SALES 4	—	—	×	×
Customer product sales analysis	SALES 2	—	—	×	×
Product sales analysis	SALES 1	—	×	×	×
Consortium case sales listing	CONLST	—	—	×	×
Product case sales listing	STOCK	—	—	—	×
Customer profile listing	END1	—	—	×	×
Month and year-end file reset	END2	—	—	×	×

18. Processing indicators. The internal codes which indicate the current state of processing an order are listed below.

$\emptyset$—Order number not yet used.
1—Order entered: picking list to be printed.
2—Picking list printed: waiting for amendment.
3—Picking list amended: ready to invoice or credit.
4—Invoiced and complete.

5—Order cancelled.

1 and 2 can be bypassed if no picking list is required.

19. Start of day pre-processing routine. Before processing can commence it is necessary to set up the computer system and the following steps indicate the routine to be followed.

(*a*) Switch on power on processor and disc drives.

(*b*) Load disc packs—master on drive ∅—workfile on drive 1.

(*c*) Prepare workstation for use by obtaining conversational loader (operating system).

(*d*) Message received "enter program name".

(*e*) In response to "enter program name", load the program "setcom" (clears processors memory). The sequence of steps is as follows.

(*i*) Select and enter—SETCOM (depress ENTER key).

(*ii*) Select and enter—START UP (depress space key). CLEAR = SYSTEM (depress ENTER key).

(*iii*) Select and enter—LOAD (depress space key)—LIOCS (depress ENTER key).

(*iv*) Select and enter—SET (depress space key) DATE = YY/MM/DD (depress ENTER key).

(*v*) Depress control key no. 1 (CTL1).

(LIOCS: This program loads the disc handling routines—software).

(*vi*) Message received "enter program name".

(*vii*) In response to "enter program name" load the program "date". The sequence of steps is as follows: enter date as DDMMYY; DDMMYY (date entered). (The date will be printed on all output listings.)

(*viii*) Switch on power on line printer and obtain the conversational loader on the V.D.U.s.

20. Order entry routine—VDORDS. Details of orders are entered on-line by means of a V.D.U. The operator enters order details as required from price list order forms (P.L.O.F.s) (*see* Fig. 56). The details are entered on an interactive basis in response to questions asked by the system which are displayed on the screen of the V.D.U. The routine is outlined in Fig. 57 which shows the order entry operating instructions. The layout of the screen is shown in Fig. 58 and the structure of the order entry routine is shown in Fig. 59.

Information for each order is stored on the orders file and when entered the process indicator is converted to "1".

OPERATING INSTRUCTIONS

Program: VDORDS	Partition: ANY	Printer/Stationery NO	Drive 0: VOLTMASTER	Drive 1:

Description:

ORDER ENTRY PROGRAM (WORKSTATION OR V.D.U.)

Imput Files: FOR FILE, PRODCT. PRODUC (INDEX),
CUSTMO.CUSTOM(INDEX), CNTRCT FILE (INDEX)

Output Files: ABOVE

Operating Message:	Action:
A. ENTER PROGRAM NAME	Orders
ORDER INPUT WEEK NO. INCORRECT WEEK NUMBER.	Enter current week number. Message repeated if a bad read or invalid week.
ORDER NO.	Enter required order number or "END" to complete this order entry session (six digit order number).
ORDER RECORD NOT FOUND.	The required order number has already been used or the orders file index is out of date.
PROCESSOR INDICATOR NON ZERO.	Order number already used. Re-enter.
ACCOUNT NO.	Enter account number for this order.
DROP NO.	
CUSTOMER RECORD NOT FOUND.	Account number entered does not exist or the customer file index is out of date. If the account is valid, the customer's name and address details will fill the top half of the screen.
CUSTOMER ORDER NO.	Enter customer's order number - any ten digits. Press control key to cancel and return to a new order number.
TRANS. TYPE	Enter transaction type as follows. (a) P.L.O.F. or catering order (b) Retail supplementary. (c) Credit for current prices. (d) Drop shipment or special price deal. (e) Credit at non-current prices. Enter control key to cancel order.

FIG. 57 *Order entry (VDORDS) operating instructions.*

INVALID TRANSACTION CODE.	Enter a transaction code from the above list.
PREPICKED.	Enter "C" if complete, "P" if picking list required.
PERCENT U/L	If transaction type = 4, enter percentage uplift as 9.99 (- if discount).
(SCREEN DETAILS FILLED AND SUB-HEADINGS WRITTEN).	The cursor will now move to the sub-heading fields expecting product codes and quantity.
PRODUCT CODE	Enter six digit product code under the following rules. (a) "END" to end order. (b) Spaces for transaction type "3" allows a free form description (length twenty-five characters). (c) Valid product code.
PRODUCT RECORD NOT FOUND.	Invalid product code, re-enter.
	* As valid product code will now display the product description and pack size.
QUANTITY	Control key 10 to cancel and re-enter line with a new product code.
	Enter quantity required if product O.K.
	Enter spaces or "1" if quantity = 1.
RE-ENTER FROM QUANTITY.	Invalid quantity, re-enter.
	A quantity will automatically be negative for a credit deal.
	Quantity may be entered on a <u>case</u> basis: control key 1 = $\frac{1}{4}$ case; control key 2 = $\frac{1}{2}$ case; control key 3 = $\frac{3}{4}$ case; control key 4 = number of items.
	For a number of items out of a case, press control key 4, enter number of items required from case.
	For a case or parcel item, the cursor returns to request a new product code, maintaining the original details in the header details.

FIG. 57—*contd.*

SPLIT BUT BULK INDICATOR.	A split key has been pressed for a bulk item (e.g. bacon/cheese). Press C.T.L. 10 and re-enter product code.
PROCESS INSTRUCTION (bulk bacon only).	Enter process instruction: B = boned; D = derind; R = rolled; S = sliced; N = none.
RE-ENTER PROC.INSTR	Invalid process instruction, re-enter.
WEIGHT ORDERED (Bulk items only)	Enter weight required as six digits with two decimal places. Press enter if no weight required.
PRICE	Transaction types 4 and 5 only. Enter price required in pence with no decimal place.
V.A.T. CODE	Enter V.A.T. rate if a non-standard code or press enter for a normal code: B = not used R = standard (8 per cent) W = zero rated Y = not used.
ERROR CONDITIONS	The following error conditions preclude confirmation or order entry. Contact Head Office.
END OF FILE SYSTEM FAILURE.	End of file condition on the following files: PRODCT. PRODUC; CUSTMO.CUSTOM; CNTRCT.INDEX; FOR. FILE.
FILE SYSTEM FAILURE	Error opening any of the above files.
SYSTEM FAILURE	Error updating orders file ⎫ use Error inserting orders file ⎬ ORDIDX Error reading orders file ⎭ Error reading customer file ⎱ use Error updating customer file ⎰ CUSIDX In all cases, re-index before contacting Head Office. Suspend all operations.

FIG. 57—*contd.*

Section 1	Order input - Week No: NN Order No: NNNNNN Account No: 6 A/N Drop No: NNNN
	Name
	Address of customer } 5 lines
Section 2	Customer order No.?
	Transaction type?
	Prepicked?
Section 3	Section 1 is repeated
Section 4	Customer order No. NNNNNNNNNN Transaction type: N Prepicked: N Percent U/L: 0000
	Line number: NNNN (entered by program for order entry, entered by operator for order amendment)
	Product code?
	Description
	Pack
	Quantity?
	Process instruction? (bulkmark)
	Weight ordered? (bulkmark)
	Price
	V.A.T. code

FIG. 58   *Order entry and order amendment screen layout.*

Primary input to order processing system

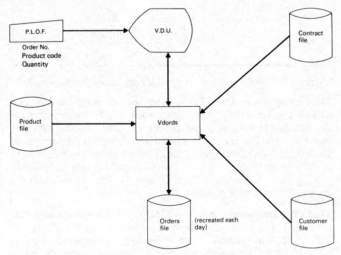

FIG. 59   *Flowchart: structure of order entry (VDORDS) routine.*

OPERATING INSTRUCTIONS

Program: PICK	Partition: 0/1	Printer/ Stationery SINGLE/ NARROW	Drive 0: VOLIMASTER	Drive 1: VOLIWORKOI

Description: Extracts order records from the orders file and writes them to an output file in preparation for sorting. This program automatically calls the sort program PSORT

Input Files: FOR. FILE

Output Files: ORDEXT. FILE

Operating Message:	Action:
ENTER PROGRAM NAME	Enter program "PICK". If a large number of orders are to be picked, the program may be run without an input device. i.e. switch partitions to run other programs. The program will scan the whole file and then call the program PSORT.
PRINTER NOT READY NO ORDERS ON FILE TO BE PICKED	Switch printer on-line or into correct partition.
CONTINUE Y/N	Enter required answer
ERROR FOUND-PROGRAM ABORTED-FOR STATUS CODE = X	
ERROR FOUND-PROGRAM ABORTED- ORDEXT STATUS CODE = X	Inform Head Office --------"--------

FIG. 60 *Order picking list (PICK) operating instructions.*

21. Picking list routine—PICK. This routine is outlined in Fig. 62 and consists of a three-program suite which continually polls the orders file searching for orders with the process indicator equal to "1". The routine is started and terminated by means of the workstation. Once picked, the process indicator is converted to "2". Operating instructions for order picking and for printing picking lists are shown in Figs. 60 and 61. Fig. 63 indicates the style and layout of a picking list.

22. Order amendment routine—VDORAM. This routine is outlined in Fig. 64 which deals with orders brought back to the V.D.U. for amendment. If an order has been entered as "prepicked" ("C") no amendment will be necessary and the order can be invoiced immediately.

OPERATING INSTRUCTIONS				
Program: PPRINT	Partition: 0/1	Printer/ Stationery YES	Drive 0: VOLIMASTER	Drive 1: VOLIWORKOI
Description: Prints picking details of all orders on the ORDSOR file				
Input Files: ORDSOR. FILE, CUSTMO. CUSTOM				
Output Files:				

Operating Message:	Action:
DO YOU WISH TO CONTINUE PICKING LIST PRINT ANSWER Y/N	"Y" will restart picking by calling program PICK "N" will end the program
ERROR FOUND STATUS CODE = X	Output on the line-printer Inform Head Office

FIG. 61 *Print picking list (PPRINT) operating instructions.*

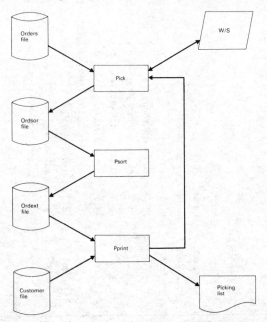

FIG. 62 *Flowchart: picking lists (PICK) routine.*

PICKING LIST

ORDER NO.	: 123457		LOAD NO. : /00			PICKER :	
CUSTOMER	: (omitted for confidentiality)					UNITAINERS :	
						DATE :	
						SHEET NO. : 001	
RACK	LINE NO.	DESCRIPTION	PACK	NUMBER	QUANTITY	QTY.PICKED	REC RETAIL
	11	GROUP MEMBERSHIP					
00	1	GRANULATED TATE & LYL SGR	15x1KG.	2			28.5
00	3	GLENRYCK PILCHARDS TOM	24x1T	1			45.0
00	4	J.W. RED SALMON	6x16OZ	1			162.0
00	5	HEINZ BAKED BEANS IN TOMT	48x50OZ	2			9.0
00	6	ROWNTREES COCOA	12x8OZ	1			99.0
00	8	K.P.WIGWAMS	36xPKT	1			7.0
00	9	I.C.I. SODA WATER SOFTENR	12x2LB	1			13.0

FIG. 63 *Picking list.*

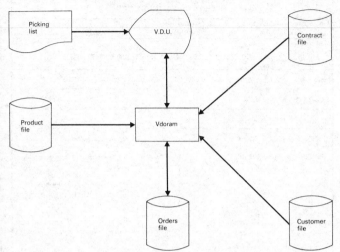

FIG. 64 *Flowchart: order amend (VDORAM) routine.*

Any picked order is likely to contain amendments for out-of-stock lines, substitutions such as change of quantity, deletions, additions and weight or price differences or changes, and the original order will require amendment. This requires the operator to quote an order number and line number (from the picking sheet) and the amended details.

Picking list orders cannot be invoiced until they have been amended. If the order does not require amendment, the order amendment program should still be used. The operator should enter "END" for the line number and reply "YES" to the question "ORDER READY FOR INVOICING?". Order amendment operating instructions are shown in Fig. 65. Once order amendments have been completed the process indicator is converted to "3".

23. Invoice and credit note production routine—INVOIC/ CREDIT. This routine is outlined in Fig. 66. The invoice and credit note production programs continually poll the orders file searching for orders with process indicator equal to "3". The routine is started and terminated by the workstation (W/S). Once invoiced, the process indicator is converted to "4".

The customer file is then updated with turnover details, etc.

OPERATING INSTRUCTIONS				
Program: VDORAM	Partition: ANY	Printer/ Stationery NO	Drive 0: VOLIMASTER	Drive 1: VOLZWORKOI

Description:

ORDER AMENDMENT, LINE DELETION OR INSERTION OF NEW ORDER LINES

Input Files: PRODCT.PRODUC, FOR.FILE, CUSTMO. CUSTOM, CNTRCT.FILE

Output Files: AS ABOVE

Operating Message:	Action:
ORDER AMEND - WEEK NO:	Input 2-digit week number.
INCORRECT WEEK NUMBER	Week number non-numeric or more than 53. Re-enter.
AMORDER NO.	Enter order number required for amendment. Enter "END" to terminate the program.
ORDER RECORD NOT FOUND.	Invalid order number not present on the orders file. Check and re-enter.
PROCESSOR INDICATOR NON AMEND.	Order number requested is not set for amendment. Check against records and alter using WSAMD if necessary. (Change field HO7 - Section 3.6).
CUSTOMER RECORD NOT FOUND	The order record called for amendment is for a customer account not found on the customer file - check! If this occurs with all orders, re-index the customer file using MAINT/USE CUSTDX.
(SCREEN FILES WITH ORDER DETAILS)	
LINE NUMBER	(a) Enter line number to be recalled for amendment. (b) Enter "IN" to insert a line to an order. (c) Enter line number to be deleted. (d) Enter "END" to end order.
PRODUCT CODE	In insert mode, proceed as for program ORDERS.
QUANTITY	(a) Enter "DE" to delete line or (b) Enter revised quantity if under amendment. (c) Press "ENTER" if no change. If deleted, cursor returns to line number.
NO DETAIL RECORD	Requested line number does not exist re-enter.

FIG. 65 *Order amendment (VDORAM) operating instructions.*

DELETED	Indicates that the requested line is deleted.
WEIGHT	Enter revised weight or "ENTER" if no change.
PRICE	Enter revised price or "ENTER" if no change.
	Returns to line number.
Order ready for invoicing? YES/NO	Enter "YES" to generate invoice, or "NO" if further amendment required.
ERROR MESSAGES:	
FILE/SYSTEMS FAILURE	Open error on any file (a) PRODCT. PRODUC; (b) CUSTMO. CUSTOM; (c) FOR. FILE; (d) CNTRCT.FILE.
SYSTEMS FAILURE	Update error, orders file in delete mode.

FIG. 65—*contd.*

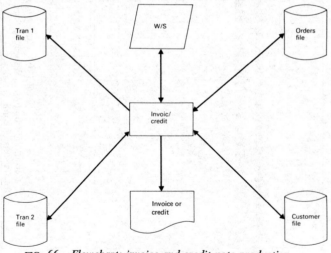

FIG. 66   *Flowchart: invoice and credit note production
(INVOIC/CREDIT) routine.*

The Tran 1 file is updated with all transactions. The Tran 2 file is updated with retail supplementaries, etc. Figs. 66–69 show specimen invoices and a credit note produced by this routine.

SALES
INVOICE
CREDIT

(Company name omitted for confidentiality)

BRANCH
REMIT TO

INVOICE TO:

QUANTITY	CODE	DESCRIPTION	PACK SIZE	UNIT PRICE	PKR	VAT RATE	RECOMMENDED RETAIL PRICE	MARGIN	TOTAL RESALE VALUE	GOODS VALUE	VAT
2		GRANULATED TATE & LYL SGR	15×1KG.							9.05	7.88
62.50		DANISH A1 GREEN BACON SIDS								8.26	31.94
1		GLENRYCK PILCHARDS TOM	24×1T							7.34	
2		JW RED SALMON	6×16OZ							10.63	
1		HEINZ BAKED BEANS IN TOMT	48×5OZ							7.30	
0.50		ROWNTREES COCOA	12×8OZ							2.16	
2		MAXWELL HOUSE ICFF (GRN)	24×2OZ								
0		K.P WIGWAMS	36×PKT								
		GROUP MEMBERSHIP								0.00	0.00
		TOTAL GOODS								39.82	39.82
00.00	PCLS	DISCOUNT 0.00								44.76	0.00
		62.50LBS BAC/CHEESE								0.00	0.00

	GOODS			CUSTOMERS GROUP No	VAT RATE		TOTAL GOODS	TURNOVER LAST PERIOD	VAT REGISTRATION No
	84.58	0.00	0.00	0.00	0.00		44.76	39.82	
TAX RATE	0.00	8.00	0.00	0.00	25.00	TOTAL TAX			
TAX	0.00	0.00	0.00	0.00	0.00		0.00		

E & O.E.

TOTAL DUE 84.58

TERMS : 1 NETT 7 DAYS
2 NETT 14 DAYS
3 NETT 30 DAYS
4 NETT 15th OF THE MONTH AFTER MONTH OF DELIVERY

All goods remain our property and are not the subject of sale or other disposal until paid for in full. Goods should be checked on arrival. We cannot accept liability for shortage unless notified to our depot.

FIG. 67 *Sales invoice (a).*
Certain information in respect of prices and margins has been omitted for reasons of confidentiality.

FIG. 68 *Sales invoice (b)*.
Certain information in respect of prices and margins has been omitted for reasons of confidentiality.

SALES
INVOICE
CREDIT

(Company name omitted for confidentiality)

INVOICE TO:

BRANCH

REMIT TO

QUANTITY	CODE	DESCRIPTION	PACK SIZE						VAT
1	160035	CORNFLAKES	7KG						3.60
1	160100	OATFLAKES	50KILO						14.00
2	137050	MARROWFAT PEAS	3KG						2.60
1	149040	BIRDS STRAWBRRY BLANCMANG	3.5KG						1.45
11.50	330b1	DELEC SHOULDERS	11.5LB						7.70
	34105	GLENRYCK PILCHARDS TOM	24×1T						9.53
0007	PCTS	TOTAL GOODS 0.00							38.88
		DISCOUNT						0.00	0.00
		11.50LBS BAC/CCHEESE						0.00	

	GOODS						TOTAL GOODS	38.88	DISCOUNT 0.00	38.88
		38.88	0.00	0.00	0.00	0.00			
	TAX RATE						TOTAL TAX	0.00	TOTAL DUE	38.88
		0.00	8.00	0.00	25.00	0.00			
	TAX								
		0.00	0.00	0.00	0.00	0.00			

E & O. E.

TERMS: 1 - NETT 7 DAYS
2 - NETT 14 DAYS
3 - NETT 30 DAYS
4 - NETT 1st OF THE MONTH AFTER MONTH OF DELIVERY

FIG. 69 Sales credit note.

INVOICE TO:

SALES (c) (Company name omitted for confidentiality)

INVOICE
CREDIT

BRANCH

REMIT TO

ACCOUNT No DROP No	INVOICE REF	INVOICE DATE	TAX POINT	LOAD No	TERMS		CUSTOMERS ORDER No	TURNOVER LAST PERIOD		VAT REGISTRATION No

QUANTITY	CODE	DESCRIPTION	PACK SIZE	UNIT PRICE	PER	VAT RATE	RECOMMENDED RETAIL PRICE	% MARGIN	TOTAL RESALE VALUE	GOODS COST Discountable	GOODS COST Nondiscountable	VAT
1	1	CREDIT RE CHEESE		4.56		0					4.56 —	
		TOTAL GOODS VALUE								0.00	4.56 —	
		******CREDIT NOTE******CREDIT NOTE******CREDIT NOTE******CREDIT NOTE******										

TERMS 1—NETT 7 DAYS
2—NETT 14 DAYS
3—NETT 30 DAYS
4—NETT 14th OF THE MONTH AFTER MONTH OF DELIVERY

All goods on this invoice are hereby guaranteed to be of the nature substance and quality described and to conform in every respect with the Food and Drugs Act and all regulations relating to the sale of Food now in force. Goods should be examined upon delivery. Particulars of any damage or shortage notified to our driver.

Any further claims must be made within 24 hours of time of delivery.

GOODS	4.56 —	0.00	0.00	0.00
TAX RATE	0.00	8.00	0.00	25.00
TAX	0.00	0.00	0.00	0.00

TOTAL GOODS	0.00	4.56 —		
TOTAL TAX	0.00	TOTAL DUE	4.56 —	

E & O.E.

FIG. 69 *Sales credit note.*

24. File security routine—COPYD. To avoid the consequences of the system failing due to files becoming corrupted or accidentally erased this routine provides for files to be copied. The system may then be recovered by using file copies when necessary. The routine is outlined in Fig. 70.

25. Retail sales ledger routine—RETAIL. The company profile (*see* **1**) stated that the sales ledger posting routine was a clerical operation. This routine prints out details of sales to customers providing information for posting to the sales ledger manually. The routine is outlined in Fig. 71 and the print-out shown in Fig. 72.

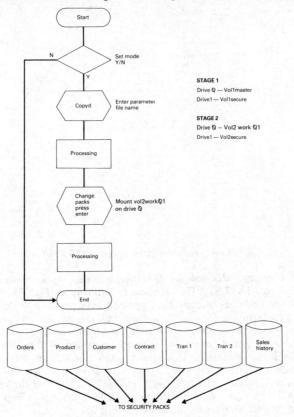

FIG. 70 *Flowchart: file security (COPYD) routine.*

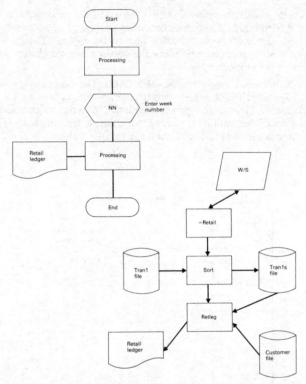

FIG. 71 *Flowchart: retail sales ledger (RETAIL) routine.*

26. Catering sales ledger—daily/weekly sales report routine—ACT inc. INVLST. This routine is outlined in Fig. 73. The TRAN 1 file has already been updated with transaction details and the customer file with turnover details (*see* invoice and credit note production routine, *see* Fig. 66). A print-out is produced for catering accounts to enable sales to be posted to the catering sales ledger manually. In addition, sales reports are produced which are initially classified by representative (*see* Figs. 74–76), and then by customer type (*see* Figs. 77–79). Note that the value of sales in Figs. 74–76 correspond with those shown in Figs. 77 and 78 and which are summarised in Fig. 79.

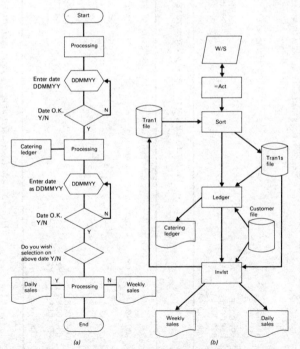

```
                    RETAIL SALES LEDGER
○                                                          ○
○    ACCOUNT    Y2A456                                     ○
○    WEEK NO.   :   17                                     ○
○                                                          ○
○                                         BAL B/FWD        ○
○                                                          ○
○    REF.     DATE    GOODS    TAX     TOTAL     CASH      ○
○    123457           84.58    0.00    84.58               ○
○                                                          ○
○                     84.58    0.00    84.58               ○
○                                                          ○
○                                      CARRIED FWD         ○
○                                                          ○
```

FIG. 72   *Retail sales ledger.*

FIG. 73   *Flowchart: catering sales ledger daily/weekly sales report
(ACT INC. INVLST) routine.*

FIG. 74 Sales to customer by representative report (a).

ACC/NO.	DROP	CUSTOMER	NAME	SALES TO CUSTOMER BY REPRESENTATIVE REFERENCE	DATE	GOODS	TAX	TOTAL
A5M001		ABC		123456		38.88	0.00	38.88 B
REP CODE	A5				DEBITS	38.88	0.00	38.88
REP CODE	A5				CREDITS	0.00	0.00	0.00
REP CODE	A5				NETT	38.88	0.00	38.88

(See Figs. 68 and 77)

FIG. 75 Sales to customer by representative report (b).

ACC/NO.	DROP	CUSTOMER	NAME	SALES TO CUSTOMER BY REPRESENTATIVE REFERENCE	DATE	GOODS	TAX	TOTAL
Y2A456		XYZ		123457		84.58	0.00	84.58 B
REP CODE	Y2				DEBITS	84.58	0.00	84.58
REP CODE	Y2				CREDITS	0.00	0.00	0.00
REP CODE	Y2				NETT	84.58	0.00	84.58

(See Figs. 67, 78 and 97)

SALES TO CUSTOMER BY REPRESENTATIVE

ACC/NO.	DROP	CUSTOMER	NAME	REFERENCE	DATE	GOODS	TAX	TOTAL
Z3B765		DEF		123458		4.56-	0.00	4.56-
REP CODE	Z3				DEBITS	0.00	0.00	0.00
REP CODE	Z3				CREDITS	4.56-	0.00	4.56-
REP CODE	Z3				NETT	4.56-	0.00	4.56-

(*See* Figs. 69 and 78)

FIG. 76 *Sales to customer by representative report (c).*

SALES BY CUSTOMER TYPE

ACC/NO.	DROP	CUSTOMER	NAME	REFERENCE	DATE	GOODS	TAX	TOTAL
CONTRACT CATERING					TOTAL DEBITS	38.88	0.00	38.88
CONTRACT CATERING					TOTAL CREDITS	0.00	0.00	0.00
CONTRACT CATERING					TOTAL NETT	38.88	0.00	38.88

(*See* Figs. 68 and 74)

FIG. 77 *Sales by customer type report (a).*

SALES BY CUSTOMER TYPE

ACC/NO.	DROP	CUSTOMER	NAME	REFERENCE	DATE	GOODS	TAX	TOTAL
A. P. T.				TOTAL	DEBITS	84.58	0.00	84.58
A. P. T.				TOTAL	CREDITS	4.56-	0.00	4.56-
A. P. T.				TOTAL	NETT	80.02	0.00	80.02

(See Figs. 67, 69, 75 and 76)

FIG. 78 *Sales by customer type report (b).*

SALES SUMMARY

ACC/NO.	DROP	CUSTOMER	NAME	REFERENCE	DATE	GOODS	TAX	TOTAL
GRAND TOTAL					DEBITS	123.46	0.00	123.46
GRAND TOTAL					CREDITS	4.56-	0.00	4.56-
GRAND TOTAL					NETT	118.90	0.00	118.90

FIG. 79 *Sales summary report.*

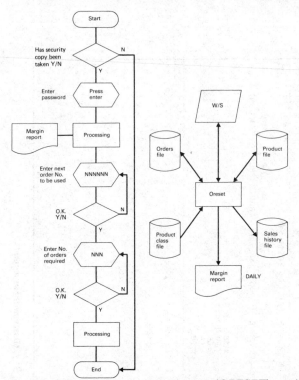

FIG. 80 *Flowchart: daily gross margin report (ORESET) routine.*

27. Daily gross margin report routine—ORESET. The purpose of this routine is the production of a gross margin report for each invoice. The routine is outlined in Fig. 80 and the layout of the report is shown in Fig. 81. Note that the sales values relate to those shown in Figs. 74–76. The detail for this report is obtained from the orders file (*see* **38**), which stores details of current orders and the sales history file (*see* **43**), which stores the cost of sales per week and period and the value of sales per week and period and to date.

28. Representatives' product sales analysis routine—SALES 3. Details of sales held on the sales history file (*see* **43**), by product class and representative code and the value of sales per week, period and to date, etc. are sorted into representative code and the various product sales by representative are printed out. The routine is shown in Fig. 82 and the print-outs in Figs. 83 and 84.

GROSS MARGIN % REALISED (PER INVOICE)

ORDER NO.	ACC.NO./DROP	*SALES VALUE (£)	COST VALUE (£)	MARGIN %	PROFIT(£)	DISCOUNT (£)
						0.00

	ORDER NO.	ACC.NO./DROP		
CUSTOMER	123456.	A5M001		38.88
	Y2A456	ORDER 123457 LINE	D000 PRICE EXT.	84.58
	123457	Y2A456		4.56-
	123458	Z3B765		118.90
		TOTALS		

VALUE POSTED TO SALES HISTORY FILE (£.P)=
118.90

TOTAL LINES INVOICED =
16

LINES NOT INVOICED-OUT OF STOCK-
1

INVOICED WEIGHTS:-   BACON   62.50   CHEESE   0.00

FIG. 81   *Gross margin report.*

* *See Figs. 74–76.*

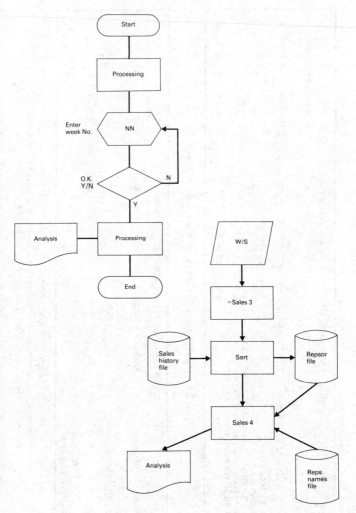

FIG. 82 *Flowchart: representatives' product sales analysis (SALES 3) routine.*

WEEKLY REPRESENTATIVES – PRODUCT SALES ANALYSIS

WEEK 17   PAGE 01

REP.	CLASS DESCRIPTION	CLASS	THIS WEEK	THIS PERIOD	-1	-2	-3	-4	-5	-6	TO-DATE	CASES
A5	CANNED MEATS	033	7.70	7.70							7.70	1
A5	CANNED FISH	034	9.53	9.53							9.53	1
A5	DEHYDRATED VEGETABLES (CAT.PKS)	137	2.60	2.60							2.60	2
A5	INSTANT DESSERTS (CAT.PACKS)	149	1.45	1.45							1.45	1
A5	CEREALS & CRISPBREAD(CAT.PK)	160	17.60	17.60							17.60	2
	GRAND TOTAL REP A5		38.88	38.88							38.88	7

(See Fig. 68)

FIG. 83   *Weekly representatives: product sales analysis.*

REPRESENTATIVE SUMMARY – PRODUCT SALES ANALYSIS

REP.CODE	REP.NAME	COST OF SALES	VALUE OF SALES	GROSS MARGIN	% OF TOTAL SALES	% OF TOTAL PROFIT	CASE SALES
A5			38.88		32.69 %	43.35 %	7
Y2			84.58		71.13 %	60.74 %	9
Z3			4.56-		3.83 % –	4.10 % –	
	TOTALS		118.90				16

(See Figs. 74-6, 83 and 89)

FIG. 84   *Representative summary: product sales analysis.*
Information in respect of representatives' names, cost of sales and gross
margin has been omitted for reasons of confidentiality.

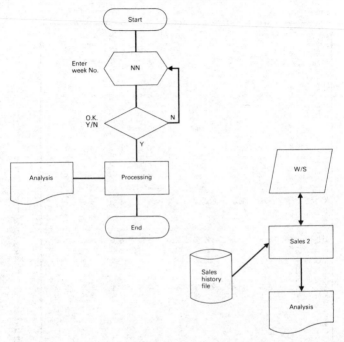

FIG. 85 *Flowchart: customer product sales analysis (SALES 2) routine.*

29. Customer product sales analysis routine—SALES 2. From details stored on the sales history file (*see* **43**), in respect of sales by product class, description, customer type and sales in respect of the current period, last period and year-to-date, etc. the customer product sales analysis is printed out. The routine is shown in Fig. 85 and the print-outs in Figs. 86 and 87.

30. Product sales analysis routine—SALES 1. From details stored on the sales history file (*see* **43**), in respect of cost and value of sales, various reports are produced for the current week and for the various periods and year-to-date. The reports include both product and departmental sales analyses as well as gross profit margins. The routine is shown in Fig. 88 and the reports in Figs. 89–92.

END OF PERIOD CUSTOMER SALES ANALYSIS
BY PRODUCT CLASS

PRODUCT CLASS	DESCRIPTION	THIS PERIOD SALES	LAST PERIOD SALES	LAST-1	LAST-2	LAST-3	LAST-4	LAST-5	YEAR TO-DATE
014	BACON AND HAMS								
21	A.P.T. FULL	31.94	0	0	0	0	0	0	31.94
TOTAL FOR PRODUCT CLASS 014		31.94	0	0	0	0	0	0	31.94
033	CANNED MEATS								
01	CONTRACT CATERING	7.70	0	0	0	0	0	0	7.70
TOTAL FOR PRODUCT CLASSNG033		7.70	0	0	0	0	0	0	7.70
034	CANNED FISH								
01	CONTRACT CATERING	9.53	0	0	0	0	0	0	9.53
21	A.P.T. FULL	17.31	0	0	0	0	0	0	17.31
TOTAL FOR PRODUCT CLASS 034		26.84	0	0	0	0	0	0	26.84
036	CANNED VEGETABLES								
21	A.P.T. FULL	7.36	0	0	0	0	0	0	7.36
TOTAL FOR PRODUCT CLASS 036		7.36	0	0	0	0	0	0	7.36
061	SUGAR								
21	A.P.T. FULL	7.88	0	0	0	0	0	0	7.88
TOTAL FOR PRODUCT CLASS 061		7.88	0	0	0	0	0	0	7.88
063	BEVERAGES								
21	A.P.T. FULL	17.93	0	0	0	0	0	0	17.93
TOTAL FOR PRODUCT CLASS 063		17.93	0	0	0	0	0	0	17.93
083	SNACKS								
21	A.P.T. FULL	2.16	0	0	0	0	0	0	2.16
TOTAL FOR PRODUCT CLASS 083		2.16	0	0	0	0	0	0	2.16
137	DEHYDRATED VEGETABLES (CAT. PKS)								
01	CONTRACT CATERING	2.60	0	0	0	0	0	0	2.60
TOTAL FOR PRODUCT CLASSNG137		2.60	0	0	0	0	0	0	2.60

FIG. 86   *End of period customer sales analysis by product class.*

END OF PERIOD CUSTOMER SALES ANALYSIS BY
CUSTOMER TYPE   WEEK: 17 PAGE: 03

		THIS PERIOD SALES	LAST PERIOD SALES	LAST-1	LAST-2	LAST-3	LAST-4	LAST-5	YEAR TO-DATE
01	CONTRACT CATERING	38.88	0	0	0	0	0	0	38.88
21	A. P. T. FULL	84.58	0	0	0	0	0	0	84.58
26	A. P. T. ASSOCIATE	4.56-	0	0	0	0	0	0	4.56-

(See Figs. 77 and 78)

FIG. 87   *End of period customer sales analysis by customer type.*
(See next page for FIG. 88.)

WEEKLY PRODUCT SALES ANALYSIS   WEEK 17 PAGE 1
DATE:

PRODUCT CLASS	CLASS DESCRIPTION	COST OF SALES	VALUE OF SALES	GROSS PROFIT MARGIN	CASE SALES
014	BACON AND HAMS		0.00		1
033	CANNED MEATS		31.94		1
034	CANNED FISH		7.70		3
036	CANNED VEGETABLES		26.84		2
061	SUGAR		7.36		2
063	BEVERAGES		7.88		1
083	SNACKS		17.93		1
137	DEHYDRATED VEGETABLES (CAT.PKS)		2.16		2
149	INSTANT DESSERTS (CAT.PACKS)		2.60		1
160	CEREALS & CRISPBREAD (CAT.PK)		1.45		2
900	ADVERTISING & MEMBERSHIP		17.60		
990	MISC. CREDITS		0.00		
			4.56-		
			118.90		**16**

(See Figs. 84 and 92)

FIG. 89   *Weekly product sales analysis.*
Cost of sales and gross profit have been omitted for reasons of confidentiality.

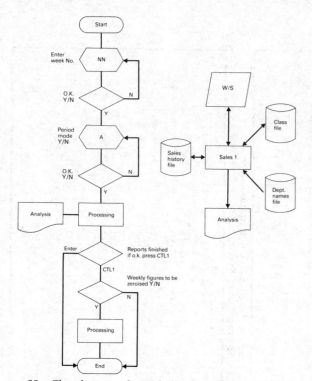

FIG. 88   *Flowchart: product sales analysis (SALES 1) routine.*

PRODUCT SALES ANALYSIS: PERCENTAGE OF TOTAL SALES AND TOTAL PROFIT		
PRODUCT CLASS	% OF TOTAL SALES	% OF TOTAL PROFIT
000	0.000 %	0.000 %
014	26.862 %	17.038 %
033	6.476 %	9.188 %
034	22.573 %	30.062 %
036	6.190 %	6.779 %
061	6.627 %	1.605 %
063	15.079 %	16.146 %
083	1.816 %	2.497 %
137	2.186 %	3.211 %
149	1.219 %	1.427 %
160	14.802 %	16.146 %
900	0.000 %	0.000 %
990	3.835 %	4.103 %

FIG. 90   *Product sales analysis: percentage of total sales and total profit.*

DEPARTMENT ANALYSIS OF PRODUCT SALES

DEPT. NO.	DEPARTMENT	COST OF SALES	VALUE OF SALES	GROSS PROFIT	% OF TOTAL SALES	% OF TOTAL PROFIT	CASE SALES
01	PROVISIONS		31.94		26.86 %	17.03 %	1
P	NOT FOUND		0.00		0.00 %	0.00 %	
05	GROCERY FOOD		69.87		58.76 %	66.28 %	10
09	CATERING FOOD		21.65		18.20 %	20.78 %	5
15	ADVERTISING/MEMBERSHIP		0.00		0.00 %	0.00 %	
16	MISCELLANEOUS CREDITS		4.56—		3.83 %—	4.10 %—	
			118.90				16

FIG. 91 *Product sales: department analysis.*

Cost of sales and gross profit have been omitted for reasons of confidentiality.

PERIOD PRODUCT SALES ANALYSIS

DATE :

PROD. CLASS	DESCRIPTION	THIS PER COST	THIS PER SALES	GROSS %	LAST PER SALES	LAST-1 SALES	LAST-2 SALES	LAST-3 SALES	LAST-4 SALES	LAST-5 SALES	TO DATE SALES (£)	CASE SALE
014	BACON AND HAMS	0.00	31.94								31	1
033	CANNED MEATS		7.70								7	1
034	CANNED FISH		26.84								26	3
036	CANNED VEGETABLES		7.88								7	2
061	SUGAR		2.16								7	2
063	BEVERAGES		17.93								17	1
083	SNACKS		2.60								2	1
137	DEHYDRATED VEGETABLES (CAT.PKS)		1.45								2	1
149	INSTANT DESSERTS (CAT.PACKS)		17.60								1	2
160	CEREALS & CRISPBREAD (CAT.PK)		0.00								17	2
900	ADVERTISING & MEMBERSHIP											
990	MISC. CREDITS		4.56—								4	2
			118.90								118	16

(*See* Fig. 89)

FIG. 92 *Period product sales analysis.*

Cost of sales and gross profit have been omitted for reasons of confidentiality.

31. Consortium case sales listing routine—CONLST. From details stored on the product file (*see* **40**), a list is printed in respect of consortium case sales for the current period. The routine is shown in Fig. 93.

32. Product case sales listing—STOCK. Also from details stored on the product file a list is printed in respect of catering and retail case sales since week 1. The routine is outlined in Fig. 94 and the list in Fig. 95.

33. Customer profile listing—END 1. From details stored on the customer file (*see* **39**), details of customers are printed out in respect of customer type (*see* **8**), sales this period, last period, goods to date and discount received to date. The routine is shown in Fig. 96 and the list in Fig. 97.

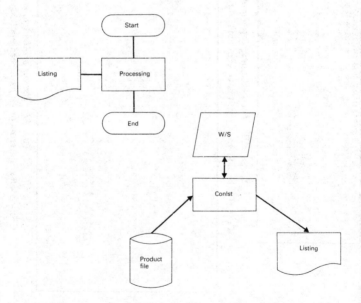

FIG. 93   *Flowchart: consortium case sales listing (CONLST)*
routine.

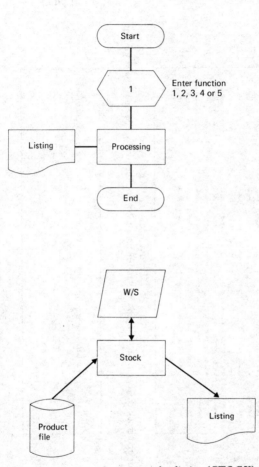

FIG. 94 *Flowchart: product case sales listing (STOCK) routine.*

PRODUCT CASE SALES LIST

PROD.CODE	DESCRIPTION	PACK SIZE	LOCATION	SUPPLIER	CURRENT STOCK	UNIT COST	STOCK COST	CATERING SALE QTY	RETAIL SALE QTY
006148	T-LAMBERT&BUTLER INT.	10x20	T00	000000	99999			000000	000000
006152	T-SLIM KINGS	10x20	T00	000000	99996			000000	000003
006161	T-SOLENT FILTER	10x20	T00	000000	99998			000000	000001
006171	T-SOLENT FILTER	10x20	T00	000000	99998			000001	000000
006181	T-WILLS 200 WOODBINES	20 x 10's	T00	90956	95757			000067	000876
006191	T-WILLS 200 WOODBINES	10 x 20's	T00	90956	95844			000020	000971
006211	T-WILLS 200 WOODBINS FLT/T	10 x 20's	T00	90956	99814			000000	000014
006213	T-BELAIR NO COUPONS	10x20's	T00	000000	99441			000000	000113
006215	T-EMBASSY ENVOY NO COUPON	10x20's	T00	000000	99916			000000	000066
006216	T-EMBASSY NO.5 EX.MILD	10x20	T00	000000	99992			000000	000007

FIG. 95 *Product case sales list.*

Unit cost and stock cost values have been omitted for reasons of confidentiality. (*See next page for Fig. 96.*)

CUSTOMER PROFILE LISTING

ACCOUNT DROP CUSTOMER NAME	TYPE	MAIN	SUPP.	THIS PER	LAST PER	TO DATE	GOODS TO DATE	DISC TO DATE
Y2A456	21	1	0	84.58	0.00	84.58	84.58	0.00
Y2T513	26	0	0	0.00	0.00	0.00	0.00	0.00
Y2W678	21	0	0	0.00	0.00	0.00	0.00	0.00
SUB TOTALS		1	0	84.58	0.00	84.58	84.58	0.00

FIG. 97 *Customer profile listing.*

34. Month and year end file reset routine—END 2. This routine is shown in Fig. 98.

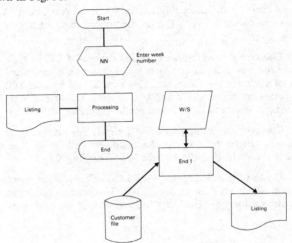

FIG. 96 *Flowchart: customer profile listing (END 1) routine.*

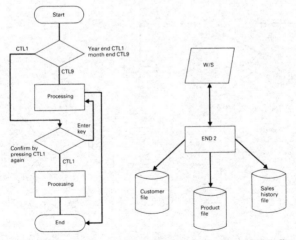

FIG. 98 *Flowchart: month and year end file reset (END 2) routine.*

DATA REPORTS

In addition to the preceding routines various processing operations are concerned with the production of data reports as follows.

35. Contract product/customer listing routine—CLIST. This routine produces a list of products on contract showing prices and list of customers on contract. This is achieved by accessing the customer, product and contract files (*see* **39**, **40** and **42**). The routine is shown in Fig. 99 and the listing in Fig. 100.

36. Customer file listing routine—CULIST. The customer file listing is produced by accessing the customer file (*see* **39**). The routine is shown in Fig. 101 and the listing in Fig. 102.

37. Product file listing routine—PRLIST. This routine is outlined in Fig. 103 and the listing in Fig. 104. This is produced by accessing the product file (*see* **40**), and consists of a list of products

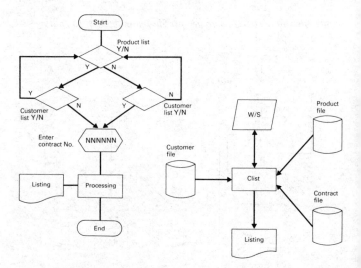

FIG. 99   *Flowchart: contract product/customer listing (CLIST) routine.*

PRODUCTS ON CUSTOMER LISTING

PROD.	DESCRIPTION	PACK	COST PRI.	RETAIL PRI.	CATER PRI.	CONTRACT PRI.
PRODUCT CATEGORY 033 DISCOUNT/SURCHARGE 0.05				:	:	:
PRODUCT CATEGORY 004 DISCOUNT/SURCHARGE 0.05				:	:	:
131050	MARROWFAT PEAS	3KG	:	:	:	:
149040	BIRDS STRAWBRRY BLANCMANG	3.5KG				
149050	BIRDS VANILLA BLANCMANGE	3.5KG				
153180	PATNA RICE	7 LB				
160035	CORNFLAKES	7KG				
160100	OATFLAKES	50KILO				

FIG. 100 *Products on contract listing.*
Prices have been omitted for reasons of confidentiality.
(*See next page for* FIG. 101.)

CUSTOMER FILE LISTING BY LEDGER PREFIX

NAME AND ADDRESS	REP.	TYPE	AREA	LOAD	DISC-A	DISC-B	DISC-INV	@	MINVAL	SORT-CODE
A5M001	A5	01	00		0.00	0.00	0.00	£	0.00	0
A5R123	A5	01	00		0.00	0.00	0.00	£	0.00	0
TESTER		01	00		0.00	0.00	0.00	£	0.00	0
X1S126	X1	10	00		0.00	0.00	0.00	£	0.00	0

FIG. 102 *Customer file listing by ledger prefix.*
Name and address details have been omitted for reasons of confidentiality.

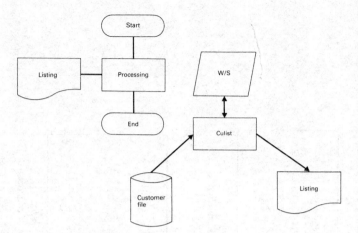

FIG. 101 *Flowchart: customer file listing (CULIST) routine.*

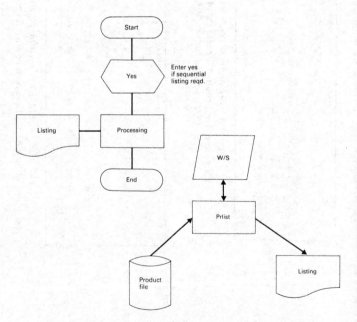

FIG. 103 *Flowchart: product file listing (PRLIST) routine.*

PRODUCT FILE LISTING

CODE	DESCRIPTION	PACK	R.UNIT	VAT	LOCTN	REC.RSP	COST	CATERING	RETAIL	P/C MRKUP	P/C PROFIT	PER	SPLT	DIS
006136	T-EMBASSY ULTRA MILD	10x20	10	R	TOO							CASE	05	0
006146	T-GOLD FLAKE	10x20	10	R	TOO							CASE	05	0
006148	T-LAMBERT&BUTLER INT.	10x20	10	R	TOO							CASE	05	0
006152	T-SLIM KINGS	10x20	10	R	TOO							CASE	05	0
006161	T-SOLENT FILTER	10x20	10	R	TOO							PACK	05	0
006171	T-SOLENT FILTER	10x20	10	R	TOO							CASE	05	0
006181	T-WILLS 200 WOODBINES	20 x 10's	20	R	TOO							PACK	00	0
006191	T-WILLS 200 WOODBINES	10 x 20's	10	R	TOO							PACK	00	0
006211	T-WILLS 200 WOODBNS FLT/I	10 x 20's	10	R	TOO							PACK	00	0
006213	T-BELAIR NO COUPONS	10 x 20's	10	R	TOO							CASE	05	0
006215	T-EMBASSY ENVOY NO COUPON	10 x 20's	10	R	TOO							PACK	55	0

FIG. 104 *Product file listing.*
Certain details have been omitted for reasons of confidentiality.

showing data elements in respect of recommended retail selling price, cost, percentage mark up and profit, etc.

SYSTEM MASTER FILES

38. Orders file. This file is created during the order entry (VDORDS) routine (*see* **20**). The structure of the file is as follows:

    (*a*) order number—reset by order reset program;
    (*b*) process indicator—0;
    (*c*) order number—via V.D.U.⎫ reset by order entry program.
    (*d*) line number   ⎬

Then follow details extracted from the customer file:

    (*a*) customer account number;
    (*b*) customer name;
    (*c*) representative code;
    (*d*) customer type.

These details are then followed by data extracted from the product or contract file:

    (*a*) product code or class;
    (*b*) product description;
    (*c*) pack size;
    (*d*) location code;
    (*e*) cost price;
    (*f*) selling price—as appropriate;
    (*g*) recommended retail selling price;
    (*h*) V.A.T. code;
    (*i*) discount indicator;
    (*j*) bulkmark;
    (*k*) split pack indicator.

The quantity of the particular product is entered via the V.D.U.

39. Customer file. The following elements constitute the structure of this file:

    (*a*) account number;
    (*b*) name and address;
    (*c*) representative code;
    (*d*) customer type (*see* **8**);
    (*e*) turnover to date, since week 1;
    (*f*) turnover this period;

(g) turnover last period;

(h) total goods to date, since week 1;

(i) number of orders to date, since week 1;

(j) fixed discount percentage off group "A" or "B" products;

(k) fixed discount percentage off invoice;

(l) minimum value to receive above discount;

(m) contract number;

(n) discount received to date, since week 1;

(o) total turnover since last main order.

40. Product file. The structure of this file is as follows:

(a) product code;

(b) product description;

(c) pack size;

(d) number of retail units, used to calculate retail margin;

(e) wholesale price factor, used for invoice extension (*see* **9**);

(f) V.A.T. code (*see* **16**);

(g) location code (*see* **10**);

(h) bulkmark (*see* **11**);

(i) recommended retail selling price;

(j) cost price;

(k) selling price—catering;

(l) selling price—retail;

(m) discount indicator (*see* 15);

(n) case sales—catering, since week 1;

(o) case sales—retail, since week 1;

(p) case sales—consortium, this period.

41. Product class file. The structure of this file is simply:

(a) product class number;

(b) department code;

(c) product class description.

42. Contract file. The structure of this file is as follows:

(a) contract number;

(b) product number or product class;

(c) price, if product number; or

(d) percentage to surcharge (−) or to discount (+), if product class.

43. Sales history file. This file contains the following elements:

(a) key of product class—customer type—representative code;
(b) product class description;
(c) cost of sales per week and period;
(d) value of sales per week—period—to date;
(e) department code;
(f) case quantities per week and period.

OVERVIEW OF CASE STUDY V

This is to enable the reader to check what has been learnt of systems design from this case study and as a basis for review:

(a) requirements of proposed on-line order processing system;
(b) structure of interactive computer configuration;
(c) primary input to the system;
(d) elements of system in respect of:
   (i) customer types;
   (ii) calculation of wholesale price factor;
   (iii) commodity location codes;
   (iv) transaction types;
   (v) pricing of commodities;
   (vi) calculation of retail margin;
   (vii) discounts off invoice;
   (viii) V.A.T. codes;
(e) summary of processing routines, program names and frequency of processing;
(f) use of process indicators;
(g) start of day pre-processing routine;
(h) order entry routine;
(i) picking list routine;
(j) order amendment routine;
(k) invoice and credit note production routine;
(l) file security routine;
(m) retail sales ledger routine;
(n) catering sales ledger routine;
(o) daily gross margin report routine;
(p) representative product sales analysis routine;
(q) customer product sales analysis routine;
(r) product sales analysis routine;
(s) consortium case sales listing routine;
(t) product case sales listing routine;
(u) customer profile listing routine;
(v) system master files.

Examination Technique

It is important for the student to appreciate that the case studies contained in this book are designed to portray the extent to which the features of systems must be specified when they are being developed, consequently the subject matter is quite detailed. This is mentioned because some examining bodies (e.g. The Institute of Administrative Management) adopt mini-case studies which are not so detailed as the case studies in this book. The case study paper is presented to candidates at the time of the examination and 10 minutes are allowed to read the paper prior to attempting an answer.

Examination candidates are advised to read the case study through carefully at least twice, making rough notes during the process on a separate sheet of paper in respect of details relevant to the requirements of the questions asked in the case study. Such case studies often provide environmental details in respect of the type of business engaged in, details of turnover, company policy, problems, the extent of competition, and so on. Such details may be directly relevant to answering the questions asked or they may predominantly be background details.

The questions asked may relate to the sphere of systems design or data processing requiring an indication of the activities suitable for computer processing and requiring the preparation of outline flowcharts of the processes involved clearly showing inputs and outputs. In addition, questions may relate to the measures which may be taken to improve the trading and profitability of the business. In such cases candidates need to consider the case study from a corporate strategy or managerial problem solving point of view indicating courses of action which may be taken to improve the situations disclosed.

The case studies in this book are basically concerned with the design of business data processing systems rather than business problems of the type outlined above. These points are indicated to ensure that examination candidates are quite clear in their mind about the type of problem they are to deal with, whether it is of a purely systems nature or one of a managerial nature.

The guidelines which are summarised below are primarily for students concerned with examinations involving case studies relating to data processing and systems design.

(*a*) Read the case study through carefully twice.

(*b*) Note relevant points on a sheet of paper.

(*c*) Develop an answer from the points listed under appropriate headings:

(*i*) Outline of computer configuration relevant to the processing technique being suggested (e.g. batch or on-line);

(*ii*) Layout of computer input media, (e.g. a punched card);

(*iii*) Details of file structure—composition of records;

(*iv*) Layout of output reports;

(*v*) General system features which may be portrayed by means of a block diagram;

(*vi*) Sequence of processing operations which may be depicted on a computer run chart;

(*vii*) Checks and controls to be incorporated in the system.

Other examining bodies (e.g. The Institute of Marketing) present case study material to examination candidates a number of weeks prior to the examination. Candidates are allowed to pre-prepare notes in respect of the case study analysing various aspects of the information supplied. This material may be taken into the examination room where the candidates are provided with additional information and questions in respect of the case study.

Candidates may use the prepared material to answer the questions if relevant, otherwise answers must be developed at the time of the examination if the prepared material proves to be unsuitable. The paper requires the candidates to make a practical and reasoned evaluation of the problems indicated in the case material. This is, of course, pertinent to providing an answer to any type of case study.

Index

Acknowledgment, 104, 105
Advance of wages, 67
Annual holiday pay, 67
Audit controls, 44

Backing storage, *see* Master file
Batch controls, 43
Batch processing, 18–20, 104–13
Batch totals, 12, 13
Block diagram, 31, 32, 146
Bulkmark, 147
Business functions, 4
Business operations, 3, 29, 30, 46, 47, 96, 97, 142, 144
Business systems, *see* Systems

Catering sales ledger, 166, 167
Check digit verification, 12, 41–3, 76, 77
Checks and controls, 11–13, 41–4
Coding systems, 42, 102, 112, 113, 115, 116, 118, 146, 147, 149, 151
Commodity location code, 147
Company profile, 29, 30, 46, 96, 142, 144
Completed contracts, 91–5
Computer configuration, 30, 31, 48, 97, 98, 145
Computer runs, 33–41, 104, 108, 110–12, 130–4, 151–7, 159–61, 165–7, 171, 173, 175, 178, 180, 181, 183, 184, 186
Computer system
  elements of, 13, 14
  main frame, 18
  visible record, 18
Consortium case sales, 180
Contract product/customer listing routine, 184

Control element, 11–14
Controls
  audit, 44
  batch, 43
Co-operation, need for, 15
Corporate objectives, 20, 21
Corporate profile, 21
Court orders, 63, 67, 69
Credit control, 134, 137, 138
Credit notes, 159, 161, 164
Customer file listing, 184, 186
Customer master file, 116, 117, 188, 189
Customer product sales analysis routine, 175
Customer profile, 180, 182
Customer types, 146, 147

Daywork earnings, 64
Daywork rate code, 79, 80
Deductions, 66
Discount, 149
Dumping, 41, 131, 140

Environment, 21, 22
External environment, 22
Extras to contract, 87

Field checks, 44
File creation document, 71
File creation program, 71, 74
File record definition, 38, 53, 74, 75
File reset, 41, 183
Files, *see* Master file
File security, 41, 165
Fixed deductions, 66
Flowcharts, 32–5, 51, 72, 91, 99, 100, 104, 107, 131, 132, 135–9, 155, 157, 159, 161, 165–7, 171, 173, 175, 178, 180, 181, 183, 184, 186

Functions, business, 4

Hardware, *see* Computer configuration
Hash totals, 12
Holiday credit, 65, 66
Hourly paid payroll
  advance of wages, 67
  amendment to master file, 54
  annual holiday pay, 67
  court orders, 67
  creation of master file, 50
  daywork earnings, 64
  elements of, 50
  fixed deductions, 66
  holiday credit, 65, 66
  income tax, 67
  input proof sheet, 57
  machine operations, 57
  master file definition, 54
  national insurance contributions,
    employee's, 67
  net pay, 67
  note and coin analysis, 63, 64
  objectives, 49
  operator input, 54, 57
  other pay, 67
  overtime premium, 64, 65
  pay advice slip, 57–62
  payroll totals, 63
  piecework, 64
  preparation for processing, 54
  sickness holiday credit, 65, 66
  statutory holiday pay, 67
  structure of, 50
  taxable gross pay, 66

Income tax, 67
Indirect costs, 87
Input element, 7, 54–7
Input proof sheet, 56, 57, 83
Internal environment, 21, 22
Investigation, 47, 48
Invoice routine, 159, 161, 163
Invoicing run, 131–4

Job time cards, 78, 79

Labour cost card, 84
Labour costing
  check digits, 76, 77
  completed contracts, 91–5
  contract types, 74
  daywork rate code, 79, 80
  extras to contract, 87
  file amendments, 75
  file creation document, 71
  file creation program, 71, 74
  files used, 71
  indirect costs, 87
  input proof sheet, 56, 57, 83
  job time cards, 78
  labour cost input sheet, 78, 79
  machine operations, 82, 83
  objectives, 70, 71
  operator input, 82
  preparation for processing, 80
  structure of system, 71
  testing procedure, 77, 78
  updating, 83
  work in progress, 87
Labour cost input sheet, 78, 79
Limit check, 44

Machine operations, 57, 82–4
Main frame computer, 10, 18
Master file
  amendments to payroll, 54
  contract, 189
  contract, file record definition, 74
  creation of payroll, 50
  customer, 116, 117, 188
  customer, amendments, 138
  daywork rate file, file record definition, 75
  definition, payroll, 54
  file amendments, labour costing, 75
  file creation document, labour costing, 71
  file creation program, labour costing, 71, 74
  layout of records, raw material stock file, 38
  order, 115, 116, 188

Order-out file, 117
payroll, file record definition, 53
planning file, 115, 118
product, 189
sales accounting, 138–40
sales history file, 189, 190
stock, layout of records, 38
Methods
    change of, reason for, 16, 17
    determining most suitable, 17
    existing, 46, 47

National insurance contributions,
    employee's, 67
Net pay, 67
Note and coin analysis, 63, 64

Objectives
    corporate, 20, 21
    system, 21
Obsolescence, hardware, 48
On-line order processing, see Order
    processing
On-line planning, 113–15
On-line processing, 18–20, 98,
    113–15
Operating instructions, 152–4, 160,
    161
Operations, machine, 57, 82–4
Operator input, 54–7, 82–4
Order amendment, 106, 156, 159
Order entry routine, 151–5
Order index key, 102
Order master file, 115, 116
Order-out file, 117
Order processing: food wholesaling
    bulkmark, 147
    catering sales ledger routine, 166,
        167
    commodity location codes, 147
    company profile, 142
    computer configuration, 145
    consortium case sales listing rou-
        tine, 180
    contract product/customer list-
        ing routine, 184
    customer file listing routine, 184

customer product sales analysis
    routine, 175
customer profile listing, 180
customer types, 146, 147
daily gross margin report rou-
    tine, 171
discount, 149
file reset, 183
files, 145
file security routine, 165
invoice and credit note routine,
    159, 162–4
operating instructions, 152–4,
    160, 161
order amendment routine, 156
order entry routine, 151–5
picking list routine, 156–8
pre-list order form (P.L.O.F.),
    143
pre-processing routine, 151
pricing, 148
processing indicators, 151
processing routines, 146
product case sales listing, 180
product file listing routine, 184
product sales analysis routine,
    175
program names, 150
proposed system, 144
representatives' product sales
    analysis routine, 171
retail margin, 149
retail sales ledger routine, 165
sales reports and analyses,
    168–70, 172, 174, 176–9, 182
system input, 145
system output, 145, 146
transaction types, 147, 148
V.A.T. codes, 149
wholesale price factor, 147
Order processing: steel making
    accounts exceeding credit limit,
        113
    application outline, 96, 97
    batch processing, 104–13
    "bit" setting, 112, 113
    company profile, 96

Order processing: steel making—*contd.*
  computer configuration, 97, 98
  customer documentation, 111
  customer file, 116, 117
  order index key, 102
  order master file, 115, 116
  Order-out file, 117
  order pro-forma, 101
  order value calculation, 112, 113
  pricing desk, 101
  reasons for converting to on-line, 97
  routine, 98–113
  sales accounting, 130–40
  sales desk, 101, 102
  security file, 117
  system input (screen 2), 98, 99, 100
  termiprinter, 102
  video screens, 102, 114, 115, 119–30
  works documentation, 111, 112
Order pro-forma, 101
Orders file, 188
Organisation structures, 3
Output element, 10, 11
Overdue file, 140
Overtime premium, 64, 65

Pay advice slip, 57–62
Payroll, *see* Hourly paid payroll
  totals, 63
  weekly salaries, 48, 68
Picking list routine, 156–8
Piecework, 64
Planning files, 115, 118, 119
Pre-list order form (P.L.O.F.), 143, 144
Pre-processing routine, 151
Pricing, 148
Pricing desk, 101
Priorities, *see* System priorities
Processing
  batch, 18–20
  element, 8
  indicators, 151
  on-line, 18–20

preparation for, 54, 80, 83
Processing indicators, 151
Product case sales, 180–2
Product file listing, 184, 186, 187
Product sales analysis, 175, 177–9
Punched card layout, 36
Purpose of systems, 16

Raw material
  product analysis, 40
  stock file, 39
  stock schedule, 39
Raw material stock control and
  cost control
  audit controls, 44
  batch controls, 43
  block diagram, 31, 32
  check digit verification, 41–3
  checks and controls, 41
  computer configuration, 30, 31
  computer runs, 33–41
  current system, 29
  field checks, 44
  file dumping, 41
  limit check, 44
  master files, 33–5, 38, 39
  proposed system, 29, 30, 31
  raw material product analysis, 40
  raw material stock schedule, 39
  system flowchart, 32, 33
  type of business, 29
Reports
  completed contracts, 93–5
  cost review, 85, 86
  customer profile listing, 182
  customer sales by product class, 176
  gross margin, 172
  picking list, 158
  product case sales list, 182
  product file listing, 187
  product sales analysis, 173–5, 178, 179
  products on contract listing, 185
  raw material product analysis, 40
  raw material stock schedule, 39

sales, customer by representative, 168, 169
sales, customer type, 169, 170, 177
sales summary, 170
work in progress control, 88, 90
Retail margin, 149
Retail sales ledger, 165, 167
Run testing, 77

Sales accounting
balancing runs, 130, 131
credit control balances, 134, 137
customer master file amendments, 138
end of week routines, 138
invoicing run, 131–4
miscellaneous sales, 134–6
Sales department, 98
Sales desk, 101, 102
Sales ledger, 140
Sales master, 139, 140
Screens, see Video
Security file (realdumpfile), 117
Sickness holiday credit, 65, 66
Source documents, 7, 55, 78, 79, 82, 144, 145
Standards of performance, 24, 25
Statutory holiday pay, 67
Stock control system, see Raw material stock control and cost control
Storage element, 8–10
Sub-routines, video, 120–8
Sub-systems, 6, 7
System flowcharts, see Flowcharts
System objectives, 20, 21, 70, 71
System priorities, 23, 24
System problems, 23
Systems
business, 3, 4
current, 23
design, 15
elemental framework of, 7–14
flowchart, see Flowcharts
objectives, 20, 21, 70, 71
priorities, 23, 24
problems, 23
proposed, 31, 144
purpose of, 16
relationships, 5
resources, 4
sales, 9
structure of, 4, 5
sub-systems, 6, 7
types of, 6
wages, 9
Systems design, 15, 16

Taxable gross, 66
Termiprinter, 102
Testing procedure, 77, 78
Transaction types, 147, 148

Updating, 9, 37, 40, 54, 57, 71, 84, 138, 161

V.A.T., 149
Video
keyboard layout and light displays, 129
operating instructions, 128, 130
operating the, 130
screens, 102, 114, 115, 119–30
Visible record computer (V.R.C.), 10, 18
Visual display unit, see Video

Wages system, see Hourly paid payroll
Weekly salaries, 68
Wholesale price factor, 147
Work in progress, 87